English Literature: A Very Short Introduction

VERY SHORT INTRODUCTIONS are for anyone wanting a stimulating and accessible way into a new subject. They are written by experts, and have been translated into more than 45 different languages.

The series began in 1995, and now covers a wide variety of topics in every discipline. The VSI library now contains over 500 volumes—a Very Short Introduction to everything from Psychology and Philosophy of Science to American History and Relativity—and continues to grow in every subject area.

Titles in the series include the following:

Jonathan Bate

ENGLISH
LITERATURE

A Very Short Introduction

OXFORD
UNIVERSITY PRESS

OXFORD

UNIVERSITY PRESS

Great Clarendon Street, Oxford OX2 6DP

Oxford University Press is a department of the University of Oxford.
It furthers the University's objective of excellence in research, scholarship,
and education by publishing worldwide in

Oxford New York

Auckland Cape Town Dar es Salaam Hong Kong Karachi
Kuala Lumpur Madrid Melbourne Mexico City Nairobi
New Delhi Shanghai Taipei Toronto

With offices in

Argentina Austria Brazil Chile Czech Republic France Greece
Guatemala Hungary Italy Japan Poland Portugal Singapore
South Korea Switzerland Thailand Turkey Ukraine Vietnam

Oxford is a registered trade mark of Oxford University Press
in the UK and in certain other countries

Published in the United States
by Oxford University Press Inc., New York

© Jonathan Bate 2010

The moral rights of the author have been asserted
Database right Oxford University Press (maker)

First published 2010

British Library Cataloguing in Publication Data
Data available

Library of Congress Cataloging in Publication Data
Data available

Typeset by SPI Publisher Services, Pondicherry, India
Printed in Great Britain by
Ashford Colour Press Ltd., Gosport, Hampshire.

ISBN 978-0-19-956926-7

15

Contents

List of illustrations

English Literature

Chapter 1
Once upon a time

Beginnings, departures

Once upon a time, you had your first introduction to English
Literature. It may well have begun with the words 'Once upon a
time'. If you were a child in the 20th century, it might have gone like
this: 'Once upon a time, a very long time ago now, about last Friday,
Winnie-the-Pooh lived in a forest all by himself under the name of
Sanders.' Or this: 'Once upon a time there were four little Rabbits,
and their names were – Flopsy, Mopsy, Cotton-tail, and Peter.'

Or it might have been in verse. Perhaps you were a child in the
early 21st century, and it went like this: 'A mouse took a stroll
through the deep dark wood. / A fox saw the mouse, and the mouse
looked good' (Julia Donaldson, *The Gruffalo*, 1999). We enter the
story by entering the wood with the mouse. We are a little excited, a
little afraid: what will we find there? It is a very traditional literary
opening: 'In the midway of this our mortal life, / I found me in a
gloomy wood' (Dante, *Hell*, translated by Henry Cary, 1805). We
are embarking on a journey of self-discovery; we will meet strange
monsters (a gruffalo!), we will be tempted to stray, we will identify
ourselves with a courageous hero (a mouse!) who triumphs by
virtue of a resourceful imagination. The strong rhymes drive us
forward. We want to read on. And we probably asked to hear the
same story again the following night.

When Shakespeare's collected plays first appeared in print, the editors, who were his close friends and fellow actors, introduced them with a suggestion: 'Read him, therefore, and again, and again.' We would not want to read yesterday's newspaper again and again. Nor the thriller or romance or comic caper that we picked up at the last minute on the airport bookstall. The books that are read again and again become *literature*. Sometimes one of them will be a thriller or romance or comic caper. Or a children's story. A book may be described as a 'classic thriller' or 'classic romance' when it becomes definitive of its genre. It may be described as a 'classic' pure and simple when it transcends the limits of its genre – Charlotte Brontë's *Jane Eyre* (1847) is more than just a romance – and when it continues to be re-read in generations after its own. Dr Samuel Johnson, in his preface to Shakespeare (1765), said that the only test of literary greatness is 'length of duration and continuance of esteem'.

Why have Beatrix Potter's *The Tale of Peter Rabbit* (1902) and A. A. Milne's *Winnie-the-Pooh* (1926) passed the test of continued esteem so triumphantly? They can be re-read with pleasure through the generations because of three strengths: the storytelling, the characterization, and the quality of the writing. Extrinsic factors have assisted, notably the illustrations (Potter's own watercolours, E. H. Shepard's realization of the world of Pooh), rather as the performances of great actors have assisted in keeping alive Shakespeare's storytelling, characterization, and use of language. But it is with the crafting of the words, the believability of the characters, and the scope of the imaginary world that the student of literature begins.

The Gruffalo won prizes on its publication, sold four million copies in a decade, and in 2009 was recognized as 'best bedtime story' by means of the historical moment's primary mark of 'esteem': the public vote by telephone, text message, or internet click. Inspired by a Chinese folk tale of a fox who borrows the terror of a tiger, the story cleverly mingles the traditional and the innovative – a feature of many candidates for classic status. But in our high-speed

21st-century world, literary taste changes with great rapidity. There is no way of knowing whether or not *The Gruffalo* will achieve classic status. Dr Johnson reckoned that the necessary 'length of duration' was a hundred years. Even if we halve that time, I have to accept, writing in 2010, that any work I mention in this book that has appeared since 1960 can only be a *provisional* literary classic.

Peter Rabbit is an introduction to the kind of character that E. M. Forster in *Aspects of the Novel* (1927) called 'round'. Round characters have 'flat' ones as foils to set them off. In Peter's case, this is the role of his goody-goody sisters. Potter economically signals this in her first sentence by giving nursery rabbit names to Flopsy, Mopsy, and Cotton-tail, but a human one to their brother. Peter is neither good nor bad. He is at once naughty, adventurous, and innocent. This combination leads him into scrapes, but the reader always knows that he will be all right in the end. He is a child listener's first introduction to the picaresque hero of the type epitomized by Henry Fielding's *Tom Jones* (1749) and Tobias Smollett's *Roderick Random* (1748).

The great literary characters are at once intensely individualized and instantly recognizable as types who have counterparts in our own world. Each character in the world of Pooh Corner is given a unique voice and a highly distinctive set of characteristics, yet in every classroom and every boardroom there is an enthusiastic Tigger, a gloomy Eeyore, a pompous Owl who uses long words, a Rabbit who is forever organizing people. The same goes for the setting: the geography of the Hundred Acre Wood, based on the Ashdown Forest in Sussex, is mapped with precision and specificity in order to create a semblance of reality as a backdrop to the surreality of the animals' adventures, but it is also an archetypal setting, an Arcadia, an Eden, a place of pastoral innocence.

The iron rule of such a golden world is that the time will come when we have to leave it. English Literature's most solemnly beautiful representation of the moment of departure is the end of John Milton's *Paradise Lost* (1667):

They looking back, all th'eastern side beheld
Of Paradise, so late their happy seat,
Waved over by that flaming brand, the gate
With dreadful faces thronged and fiery arms:
Some natural tears they dropped, but wiped them soon;
The world was all before them, where to choose
Their place of rest, and Providence their guide:
They hand in hand with wand'ring steps and slow,
Through Eden took their solitary way.

Adam and Eve are 'solitary' because their act of free will in eating of the fruit of the tree of knowledge has severed them from God. But they walk 'hand in hand': we have human bonds to help us through life. For Milton, this is the moment when humankind is forced to grow up.

The House at Pooh Corner (1928) with a similar tone. Christopher Robin is going away. Milne began the first Pooh book in the vein of English humour:

> 'What does "under the name" mean?' asked Christopher Robin. 'It means he had the name over the door in gold letters and lived under it.'

Milne ends the second Pooh book in the vein of English reticence:

> Still with his eyes on the world Christopher Robin put out a hand and felt for Pooh's paw.
>
> 'Pooh,' said Christopher Robin earnestly, 'if I – if I'm not quite – – ' he stopped and tried again – 'Pooh, *whatever* happens, you *will* understand, won't you?'
>
> 'Understand what?'
>
> 'Oh, nothing.' He laughed and jumped to his feet. 'Come on!'
>
> 'Where?' said Pooh.
>
> 'Anywhere,' said Christopher Robin.

The measured pace of this dialogue, in which what is unsaid is as important as what is openly stated, would not be out of place in a novel by Evelyn Waugh or a play by Noël Coward. But, since Milne was writing for children, he cannot resist a final paragraph in the vein of English nostalgia:

> So they went off together. But wherever they go, and whatever happens to them on the way, in that enchanted place on the top of the Forest a little boy and his Bear will always be playing.

The world is all before us, but whatever happens we need to keep somewhere in our memories an enchanted place called, as William Wordsworth phrases it, 'recollections of early childhood'. In his Ode beginning 'There was a time' (1805), Wordsworth proposed that such recollections offer us 'Intimations of Immortality'. Literature begins to do its work of cheating time and death, conferring freedom through imagination, exactly at the moment when death comes into our world. Peter Pan, the boy who by refusing to grow up breaks the iron rule that we must leave the golden world, surrounds himself in Neverland with 'lost boys', which is to say dead children. The Pan figure himself is one of the most poignant types in English Literature, as illustrated by Sebastian Flyte in *Brideshead Revisited* (1945), clinging on to his teddy bear as a sign of his refusal to leave Arcadia and enter on the awfully big adventure that is life.

Schoolings

Pooh and his friends don't know where Christopher Robin is going. But we do. Though the text is not explicit, it must be boarding school. The second stage of our introduction to English Literature is likely to be the school story. Which immediately brings us to the inescapable English question of class. There is one education (or lack of it) for the poor and another for the rich. Ice-cold Lowood School, where impoverished Jane Eyre endures mental cruelty, and Dotheboys Hall, where unwanted boys are sent away to endure the mercies of Mr Wackford Squeers (*Nicholas Nickleby*, 1839), let

alone the workhouse of Dickens' preceding novel, *Oliver Twist; or, The Parish Boy's Progress* (1838): these are a world away from the English public school ethos of Thomas Hughes's *Tom Brown's Schooldays* (1857). The food is equally bad in all these establishments, but the posh boys are allowed sauces and pickles to make it palatable. Thanks to the real-life headmaster of Rugby, Dr Thomas Arnold, Flashman the bully is defeated and Tom is fashioned as both a gentleman and a muscular Christian. He

1. a & b 'The Expulsion': illustration by William Blake to the final lines of John Milton's *Paradise Lost* and Ernest H. Shepard to the end of *The House at Pooh Corner*

triumphs on the cricket field by day and remembers to say his prayers at night.

The boy who comes from respectable but not wealthy middle-class stock and whose public school education initiates him into the ruling class and its values, having overcome an upper-class bully along the way, became a stock figure in subsequent fiction aimed at middle-class readers. He nearly always has a good friend or two to help him on his way – Arthur in Tom's case, Ron and Hermione in that of Harry Potter.

During the school holidays, the public school spirit could be exercised while camping, boating, and climbing – Arthur Ransome's *Swallows and Amazons* (1930), the epitome of wholesome Englishness written by a sometime Bolshevik sympathizer who married Trotsky's secretary. The fortitude of a group of very English middle-class children is tested by extremity. In *The Lion, the Witch and the Wardrobe* (1950), C. S. Lewis's Pevensie children are evacuated from London in order to escape the Blitz, but find themselves fighting in a war against a fantasy version of the Nazi/Satanic horde. In R. M. Ballantyne's *The Coral Island* (1857), boys called Ralph and Jack put up a jolly good show when they are shipwrecked without adults on the coral reef of a Polynesian island.

Literature is as much about inverting traditions as inheriting them: in William Golding's *Lord of the Flies* (1954), boys called Ralph and Jack turn out to be savages rather than gentlemen when they are stranded on an island. By the same account, whereas the Christian allegory of the Narnia novels falls into line with the orthodox reading of Milton in C. S. Lewis's *A Preface to Paradise Lost* (1942), the *His Dark Materials* trilogy of Philip Pullman (1995–2000) is built on the heterodox reading of *Paradise Lost* that began with William Blake's *The Marriage of Heaven and Hell* (1793): 'Milton was a true Poet, and of the Devil's party without knowing it.' 'His dark materials' is a quotation from *Paradise Lost*, alluding to Lucifer's passage across Chaos from one world to another. Lyra, the name of Pullman's heroine, is a skewed allusion to Blake (Lyca is 'The Little Girl Lost' in *Songs of Experience*), as is the notion of each of us having a 'daemon' or emanation that simultaneously embodies our character and serves as our guardian spirit.

Villains and outsiders

Children's literature frequently imagines animals behaving like humans, whereas adult literature frequently shows humans behaving like animals. When characters in Shakespeare act inhumanely, they are compared to pelicans, serpents, and dogs. Ben Jonson wrote a comedy of deception called *Volpone* (1606), which means 'the fox', in which a servant called Mosca ('the fly') buzzes busily around the plot and a lawyer called Voltore ('the vulture') picks over the spoils.

Humanized animals are the exception rather than the rule in adult literature. They usually appear in allegorical or satirical works, most notably the fourth book of Jonathan Swift's *Gulliver's Travels* (1726), in which the Houyhnhnms are rational horses and the Yahoos bestial humans. Other examples include George Orwell's anti-Stalinist *Animal Farm* (1945) and Thomas Love Peacock's *Melincourt* (1817), a gentle critique on the idea of progress in which an Orang-Utan runs for parliament. Then there is the special case of Satan, who brings evil into the world in the form of a snake. But these are exceptions. Generally, if you want to meet a talking horse or bear or wolf or rabbit, you go to children's literature.

The literature of anthropomorphized animals is called 'fable'. It goes back to Aesop in ancient Greece. In a simple fable, a cocky or a wicked animal gets comeuppance. The tortoise beats the hare. Fables of this kind conform to the view of literature espoused by the prissy governess Miss Prism in *The Importance of Being Earnest* (1895): 'The good ended happily, and the bad unhappily. That is what fiction means.' Beatrix Potter's *The Story of a Fierce Bad Rabbit* (1906) is a fable, aimed at *very* young children. It is circumscribed by the moral opposition between villain ('fierce bad rabbit') and victim ('nice gentle rabbit'). The Fierce Bad Rabbit gets his just deserts when his whiskers and tail are blown off by a man with a gun. Potter reports this violent death in the detached, matter-of-fact narrative voice that made her an important influence on the style of Evelyn Waugh and Graham Greene.

Because of Peter Rabbit's greater complexity, and his naughtiness in particular, his story is more *literary* than that of the Fierce Bad Rabbit. Literature does not conform to the demands of governesses such as Miss Prism. Her creator, Oscar Wilde, knew that some of the best literature is more playful than earnest and that the most interesting characters are seldom the good ones who end happily. Shakespeare's charismatic villains such as Richard III, Iago in *Othello*, and Edmund the Bastard in *King Lear*, do end unhappily, but before doing so they offer immense rewards to actor and audience alike. What actor would rather play Malcolm than Macbeth?

The most frequently revived non-Shakespearean play on the English stage in the 18th and 19th centuries was Philip Massinger's *A New Way to Pay Old Debts* (1626), which owed its huge popularity to the character of the larger than life and wickedly lovable villain, Sir Giles Overreach, a part that every star actor wanted to play, and the prototype of the monstrously greedy speculating businessmen of Victorian fiction, such as Augustus Melmotte in Anthony Trollope's *The Way We Live Now* (1875) and Mr Merdle in Charles Dickens' *Little Dorrit* (1857).

The work of literature stands apart from the fable, the sermon, and the ethical treatise not least by virtue of its capacity to make wickedness interesting. Children's literature is full of witches, monsters, demons, werewolves, and grown-ups from whom you would be ill advised to accept a bag of sweets. Literature at its best is a song of experience, not of innocence. William Blake's 'The Lamb' (*Songs of Innocence*, 1789), with its 'Softest clothing, woolly, bright', is uninterestingly pious and distinctly twee until it is read up against the 'fearful symmetry' of its blazing counterpart, 'The Tyger' (*Songs of Experience*, 1794). As the critic William Hazlitt put it in Blake's lifetime, 'A lion hunting a flock of sheep or a herd of wild asses is a more poetical object than they' (essay on *Coriolanus* in *Characters of Shakespear's Plays*, 1817). Fiction works some of its best effects when the narrator, and thus the reader, is placed in the position of the hunted. Excitement is generated by fear, as when Jim Hawkins hears the approach of Blind Pew in Robert Louis Stevenson's thrilling adventure story:

> When we were about half-way through, I suddenly put my hand upon her arm, for I had heard in the silent frosty air a sound that brought my heart into my mouth – the tap-tapping of the blind man's stick upon the frozen road.

> (*Treasure Island*, 1883)

The most interesting characters are often outsiders of one sort or another. The most voracious young readers are lonely or only or introspective children. They readily identify with the solitary Jim Hawkins, for whom the pirates offer an alluring alternative community. Roald Dahl's James Henry Trotter, an orphan brought up by his cruel aunts Spiker and Sponge, finds his alternative community among the creatures aboard the Giant Peach, as does Harry Potter among the wizards of Hogwarts.

Part of the artistic economy of Shakespeare's *Othello* comes from the way in which the drama splits the figure of the outsider. Othello the Moor is an outsider because of his origin, but he wants to be loved by those around him, which is one definition of an insider. Iago the Venetian is born on the inside track, but wants nothing to do with love. He is the loner and the (evil) dreamer, which is one definition of an outsider.

Writers are particularly interested in outsiders because they often feel like outsiders themselves. Instead of participating in life, they watch themselves standing apart from life, making it the raw material for art. Iago's plotting is, it has often been observed, an analogue for Shakespeare's. It might seem curious to label Shakespeare an outsider, but that is how he must have felt when he entered the London theatre world without the university degree that was his fellow dramatists' badge of belonging. In all probability, he had a thick provincial accent that may have been one of the reasons why the earliest reference to him as a writer refers to him as an 'upstart crow'. Robert Louis Stevenson was so much the outsider that he spent most of his short life travelling abroad and ended it by spending six years in Samoa. Roald Dahl, of part Welsh and part Norwegian origin, never felt he really belonged in England, despite flying with the RAF during the Second World War. He wrote *James and the Giant Peach* (1961), the book that launched his career as an English children's author, when he was resident in distant New York.

The Victorian artist and writer Edward Lear was a supreme example of an outsider. Born into a large and downwardly mobile family in the Holloway district of east London, he spent most of his adult life as an exile and a nomad, travelling and painting in Europe, the Middle East, and the Indian subcontinent. One way of reading his nonsense poems is to see them as a response to a life lived among foreign languages:

> Long years ago
> The Dong was happy and gay,
> Till he fell in love with a Jumbly Girl
> Who came to those shores one day.
> For the Jumblies came in a sieve, they did, –
> Landing at eve near the Zemmery Fidd
> Where the Oblong Oysters grow,
> And the rocks are smooth and gray.

('The Dong with a Luminous Nose', 1876)

When I hear a native reader reciting Russian or Chinese or Yoruba poetry, I cannot understand a word of it, but I can take huge delight in the rhythms of the verse and the sounds of the words. A local version of a similar delight occurs when we encounter exotic place-names: hence 'the great Gromboolian plain', 'the Hills of the Chankly Bore', and 'the Zemmery Fidd'.

A different way of reading Lear's nonsense poems is to tease a narrative out of them. What do we know about the Dong? That he is a tender-hearted creature who is regarded with a mixture of fascination, fear, and loathing as somehow sub-human. That he is a lonely traveller with a nose that marks him out as abnormal and that he is yearning and searching for a lost love-object, a Jumbly Girl who is also abnormal in that her head is green and her hands are blue. 'Long years ago / The Dong was happy and gay': though the word did not have its modern meaning in the 19th century, there is a strong possibility that one of the reasons (along with epilepsy, depression, and a variety of other health problems) why Edward Lear, who hated his own bulbous nose, was a perpetual outsider in Victorian England is that he was almost certainly latently and unhappily gay.

A golden age?

'Once upon a time': it is where we begin with literature, and in all probability it is where literature began. The primitive community gathers round a fire and listens to a storyteller conjuring up the spirits of gods, ancestors, and heroes. Humankind needs stories in order to make sense of the world. Children love stories and make sense of their world by means of them. A history of children's literature is accordingly a history of literature itself. The first English classics to have been read aloud to almost all literate children (albeit sometimes in abridged form) were John Bunyan's *Pilgrim's Progress* (1678) and Daniel Defoe's *Robinson Crusoe* (1719). They belong to the era when British cultural life was being transformed by the combined influence of religious Puritanism

13

and John Locke's psychological theory of the child's mind as a blank slate written upon by education and environment. It was under exactly these influences that both literature explicitly for children and the adult novel took on recognizably modern form. By the early 19th century, there was a huge body of children's books. Even Shakespeare had been turned into stories for children, by way of Mary and Charles Lamb's novelization, *Tales from Shakespeare* (1807).

The Edwardian era of the early 20th century is usually seen as the golden age of children's literature. If the great theme of English children's literature is the passing of childhood, the expulsion from Arcadia, then the special poignancy of Edwardian writing comes from our retrospective knowledge that it belongs to the end of a long era of (relative) peace and (comparative) social stability. The Edwardians are like children playing in the sunlight before a cruel awakening. Virginia Woolf saw the pattern and used it as the structure for her novel *To the Lighthouse* (1927): the pre-war first part is about a childhood summer holiday by the seaside, the war makes a sharp break in the second part, and the third part is an adult elegy for a world that has been lost.

Edwardian children's authors themselves were not aware that the Great War was coming. They witnessed, and worried about, other changes. In *The Wind in the Willows* (1908), Kenneth Grahame plays off the rootedness of the Wild Wood inhabited by Badger against the riverbank upon which speculators and nouveau-riche stockbrokers build new villas. The old aristocratic lord of the manor has vanished: Toad Hall has been purchased by a pseudo-gentleman with a fad for fast cars. It will subsequently be taken over by working-class squatters in the form of Weasels. The book is an elegy for an ancient and settled way of life, a lost authenticity – in which people know their place and women do not have the vote. Even as we smile warmly at boastful Toad's naïve, energetic, selfish 'Poop Poop', we are supposed to react to his vulgarity in a similar way to the grounded, good-hearted gaoler's daughter:

'Toad Hall,' said the Toad proudly, 'is an eligible self-contained gentleman's residence very unique; dating in part from the fourteenth century, but replete with every modern convenience. Up-to-date sanitation. Five minutes from church, post-office, and golf-links, Suitable for----'

'Bless the animal,' said the girl, laughing, 'I don't want to TAKE it. Tell me something REAL about it. But first wait till I fetch you some more tea and toast.'

Kenneth Grahame anticipates Evelyn Waugh, whose favourite book was *The Wind in the Willows*, in his lament for the decline of the REAL gentleman, the sort of person, such as the aptly named Tony Last in Waugh's *A Handful of Dust* (1934), who does not concern himself with up-to-date sanitation and golf-links, which are the preoccupations of the parvenu and the estate agent.

There is a familiar fairy-story fantasy of social transformation. A night-tripping fairy swaps two babies in their cradles; a foundling child turns out to be a princess; the glass-slipper fits on Cinderella's foot. The late Victorian and Edwardian version of this story imagines a commoner becoming an aristocrat. There were many historical examples of intermarriage between old families with status and estates but little cash and the new money of either the urban industrialist or the American heiress. The brilliance of Henry James's *The Portrait of a Lady*, published in 1881, comes from the way in which Isabel Archer shows that she is a spiritual lady by *refusing* to marry Lord Warburton and become a nominal lady. A few years later, the Anglo-American novelist Frances Hodgson Burnett (who had previously written adult novels about poverty, class conflict, and marital strife) wrote her first children's story, *Little Lord Fauntleroy* (published in magazine serialization in 1885, and in book form in 1886). Little Cedric Erroll lives in Brooklyn in genteel poverty, with his widowed mother. An English lawyer arrives. He is called Havisham, the name an immediate indication that Cedric has Great Expectations.

Sure enough, the child is told that he is heir to a Lordship and a great estate in England. The book made its author into the highest-earning woman in America. Millions of copies were sold, it was translated into dozens of languages, and dramatized on stage and screen. It also became a merchandizing phenomenon. In both England and America, late Victorian mothers dressed their sons in Fauntleroy costumes.

Like many writers, Burnett was an unconventional woman. Born in England, she married an American and crossed the Atlantic. She had a very public love affair, divorced her husband, and then married an Englishman. She put her work before her family and was often away from home. Doubly caught not only between two nations, but also between two worlds, those of her imagination and her maternal duty, she was devastated when she lost one of her sons to tuberculosis at the age of fifteen. The recovery of the sick child, Colin, in *The Secret Garden* (1911) is a compensatory fantasy inspired by this bereavement. Burnett's surviving son suffered the fate of A. A. Milne's Christopher Robin: he always resented his mother for using him as the model for Little Lord Fauntleroy. The perennial cry of the lovers, friends, and relations of writers is that they have found themselves used as raw material, transmuted, not always flatteringly, into art at the expense of life.

The Secret Garden was inspired by a walled garden in Kent, where Burnett spent some of her happier years playing the part of an English country lady. But the book was written in America. Pastoral England is seen more clearly from abroad. In the story, Mistress Mary, the little girl who is used to being spoilt, is a child of empire. She comes to the house on the moors from India, a second world that was a powerful background force in much fiction of the time. She is cured of her sickliness by Dickon, the child of nature she meets in the secret garden. The interplay of realism, in which social status plays a major part, and romanticism, in which a mystical relationship with the natural world brings spiritual fulfilment, is one of the creative tensions at the heart of English Literature.

'What should they know of England who only England know?'

In August 1900, Rudyard Kipling, child of the Raj, a wanderer and a witness of the Boer War, came to live in England. He discovered Bateman's, a solid Jacobean house in a valley of the Weald down the hill from Burwash village in East Sussex. Resistant to snobbery and social pretension, Kipling was the very antithesis of Mr Toad. He would later refuse both a knighthood and the Poet Laureateship. He always insisted that Bateman's was not a manor house but the home of a successful ironmaster. Garden, oasthouses, dovecot. No park, no lodge at the gate, no long driveway 'or nonsense of that kind'.

Kipling explored the regional landscape: the marshes at Rye and Romney, the chalk of the South Downs, the woods and meadows of the Weald. He planted apple trees and took up bee-keeping. And he became fascinated by a local hedger. Watching this craftsman grub out a hedgerow gave Kipling 'a new respect for mankind': 'a poacher by heredity and instinct', the man was 'more "one with Nature" than whole parlours full of poets . . . a mine of wisdom about trees, hedges, plants and the Earth generally' (*Something of Myself*, 1937). In India, Kipling had asked 'what should they know of England who only England know?' ('The English Flag', in *Barrack-Room Ballads*, 1892). Now he was getting to know England himself, discovering the national past through archaeology – relics both Neolithic and Cromwellian were excavated on his land – and by tracking the changing landscape, the long history through which woodland became pasture, then timber plantation, then pasture again.

The Jungle Book (1894) and *Just So Stories* (1902) revealed Kipling as a master storyteller for children. In *Puck of Pook's Hill* (1906) and its sequel *Rewards and Fairies* (1910), he turned his newfound local knowledge into a mythology of the homeland in which he was not born. He imagined a history for young readers grounded neither in a chronology of events nor in the institutions of state, but in the geography or, better, the psychogeography of the land.

The children, Dan and Una, find a guide to this history when they perform a miniature version of Shakespeare's *Midsummer Night's Dream* in an improvised outdoor theatre in a meadow. Suddenly they hear a whistle among the alders, the bushes part like a stage curtain, and the real Puck appears. 'This is our field', says Dan defensively. I quote the following exchange at some length, not least in order to give the feel of Kipling's incomparable prose rhythms. Read it aloud. And slowly – you have to read Kipling slowly:

'Is it?' said their visitor, sitting down. 'Then what on Human Earth made you act Midsummer Night's Dream three times over, on Midsummer Eve, in the middle of a Ring, and under – right under one of my oldest hills in Old England? Pook's Hill – Puck's Hill – Puck's Hill – Pook's Hill! It's as plain as the nose on my face.'

He pointed to the bare, fern-covered slope of Pook's Hill that runs up from the far side of the mill-stream to a dark wood. Beyond that wood the ground rises and rises for five hundred feet, till at last you climb out on the bare top of Beacon Hill, to look over the Pevensey Levels and the Channel and half the naked South Downs.

... 'You've done something that Kings and Knights and Scholars in old days would have given their crowns and spurs and books to find out. If Merlin himself had helped you, you couldn't have managed better! You've broken the Hills – you've broken the Hills! It hasn't happened in a thousand years.'

'We – we didn't mean to,' said Una.

'Of course you didn't! That's just why you did it. Unluckily the Hills are empty now, and all the People of the Hills are gone. I'm the only one left. I'm Puck, the oldest Old Thing in England, very much at your service if – if you care to have anything to do with me. If you don't, of course you've only to say so, and I'll go.' . . .

Una put out her hand. 'Don't go,' she said. 'We like you.'

'Have a Bath Oliver,' said Dan, and he passed over the squashy envelope with the eggs.

The Bath Oliver and squished hard-boiled eggs provide the grounding in reality just as the fantasy takes flight. The eggs will be borrowed by Mr Tumnus, a reincarnation of Kipling's Puck, when he invites Lucy to her first Narnian tea in *The Lion, the Witch and the Wardrobe*. Lewis signals his indebtedness by naming the children from the Pevensey Levels mentioned here, as Dan and Una break open the hills and release the spirit of the land. Children's literature is stuffed with food – Ratty and Mole's picnic in *The Wind in the Willows*, the outlandish products of Mr Willy Wonka's Chocolate Factory (1964) – as if to suggest an analogy between the nourishment of the body and the book's own work in nourishing the mind. In the poorhouse, Oliver Twist is equally deprived of food and education. He is hungry for a little more gruel, a little more opportunity for imaginative flight.

Puck of Pook's Hill grants Dan and Una a sequence of visions of English history, grounded in copse and stream. We time-travel from the Bronze Age to the age of George Washington. We meet a centurion who has been on Hadrian's Wall, protecting Roman civilization against the barbarian, an imperial image evocative of India's North-West Frontier. But Kipling's principal emphasis is the reconciliation of Saxon and Norman. His England is a mongrel nation, enriched by wave upon wave of invasion and immigration, its multi-ethnic identity etched upon the very land. Through the centuries, the arrivants shed their religion and sign up instead for 'English' values of tolerance, good humour, and fair play. The sky gods of the old religions are transformed into spirits of place, mediated by a character called Hobden who is based on the old Hedger. *Puck of Pook's Hill* offers Kipling's child readers a history of secularization and integration that tells a very different national story from the one to which he contributed around the same time in the imperialist *History of England* (1911) co-authored with a professional historian called C. R. L. Fletcher, who provided a racial inflection that is now repellent.

Henry James described Rudyard Kipling as the most complete genius he had ever known. In 21st-century Britain, he is often dismissed as a myopic spokesman for imperialism. Such a dismissal can only be made by people who have not read *Kim* (1901), a novel about a boy that is as much of a 'crossover' book, of equal appeal to the young and the old, as Dickens' *Oliver Twist* or Pullman's *Dark Materials*. It is narrated in the third person but written through the eyes of Kim, the orphaned child of an Irish soldier, impoverished on the streets of Lahore. Kim undertakes a double journey, being swept up into the 'Great Game' of espionage as the British and the Russians fight for influence in Afghanistan, while at the same time following a Lama on the road to spiritual enlightenment. The choice between the way of politics and that of the spirit is a version of the dialectic of realism and romanticism, but the novel's greatest distinction comes from its vision of the abundant multicultural life of India, as witnessed (seen, heard, and smelt) on the Grand Trunk Road where 'all castes and kinds of men move . . . Brahmins and chumars, bankers and tinkers, barbers and bunnias, pilgrims and potters – all the world coming and going'.
The Lebanese-American critic Edward Said was one of the late 20th century's most influential analysts of what he saw as the symbiotic connection between the forces of *Culture and Imperialism*. Yet much the longest chapter of his 1993 book of that title is a detailed and highly sympathetic reading of *Kim*, entitled 'the pleasures of imperialism', in which it is argued that the book's central meaning is Kipling's profound engagement with an India that he loved but could not properly possess.

For all Kipling's sympathetic absorption in the many cultures of India, he believed that it was his duty to bear what he infamously called 'The White Man's Burden'. He was bound to fall out of fashion when the empire disappeared. The story of English Literature in the second half of the 20th century was the reversal of his journey, the granting of a voice to the colonial subjects. V. S. Naipaul, of Indian stock by way of the West Indies, replicated Kipling's arrival at Bateman's in his account of *The Enigma of Arrival* (1987) in a settled rural community in Wiltshire. He even finds himself a hedger, close kin to Kipling's Hobden, who serves as repository of local lore.

In the Italian-Scottish-English Anthony Minghella's Oscar-winning screenplay adaptation of the Sri Lankan-Canadian Michael Ondaatje's Booker Prize-winning novel *The English Patient* (1992), the beginning of *Kim* is replayed in a postcolonial key, with a central role accorded to a Sikh bomb disposal expert called Kip who, like Kim, is born in Lahore:

THE PATIENT

You have to read Kipling slowly. Your eye is too impatient – think about the speed of his pen. (*quoting Kipling to demonstrate*) What is it? 'He sat *comma* in defiance of municipal orders *comma* astride the gun Zamzammah on her brick...'... 'The Wonder House *comma* as the natives called the Lahore Museum.'

KIP

It's still there, the cannon, outside the museum. It was made of metal cups and bowls taken from every household in the city as tax, then melted down. Then later they fired the cannon at my people *comma* the natives.

THE PATIENT

So what is it you object to – the writer or what he's writing about?

What I really object to, Uncle, is your finishing all my condensed milk. (*snatching up the empty can*) And the message everywhere in your book – however slowly I read it – that the best destiny for India is to be ruled by the British.

In the 21st century, Kipling's question is more urgent than ever: what *should* they know of England who only England know?

The faceless English Patient, Almàsy, is originally Hungarian, with aspiration to the state of post-nationality. He is Ondaatje's critique of the notion of national identity. But, with his immersion in Herodotus and Kipling, he is an embodiment of cultivated literariness. When he engages in debate about *Kim*, an act of reading and literary interpretation is contained within the narrative. Minghella's screenplay skilfully fuses two scenes in Ondaatje's novel, rather as Shakespeare often scrambled together different parts of his sources. In the book, the passage about the real history of the gun Zamzammah is inscribed on the flyleaf of a copy of *Kim* by another character, the Canadian nurse Hana. Literary writing means the rewriting of existing literature: Ondaatje answers Kipling, as Pullman answers Milton and Malorie Blackman answers Shakespeare, relocating *Romeo and Juliet* in a racially mixed dystopia (*Noughts and Crosses*, 2001).

When characters read books – Jane Eyre on her window-seat at the very beginning of Charlotte Brontë's novel, Catherine Morland devouring Gothic fiction in Jane Austen's *Northanger Abbey* (1818) – they become mirrors of the reader who is reading in the book. The escape into another world – Lewis Carroll's Alice going down the rabbit hole into *Wonderland* (1865) or *Through the Looking-Glass* (1871), the Pevensie children passing through the wardrobe – is an analogue for the reader's escape from her own mundane world into the magical realm of literature. We now need to ask what are the limits of that realm.

Chapter 2
What it is

Definitions

In one of Charles Dickens' most memorable schoolroom scenes, Mr Thomas Gradgrind, who believes in the importance of facts, asks Sissy Jupe to define a horse. She panics and struggles to find the correct answer. '"Girl number twenty unable to define a horse!" said Mr Gradgrind ... "Girl number twenty possessed of no facts, in reference to one of the commonest of animals! Some boy's definition of a horse. Bitzer, yours."' Cold-eyed Bitzer knows the facts: 'Quadruped. Graminivorous. Forty teeth, namely twenty-four grinders, four eye-teeth, and twelve incisive. Sheds coat in the spring; in marshy countries, sheds hoofs, too. Hoofs hard, but requiring to be shod with iron. Age known by marks in mouth' (*Hard Times*, 1854).

Sissy's ignorance of the correct nomenclature is ironic, since she knows horses infinitely better than Gradgrind ever will, let alone Bitzer. She is one of the circus people. She has lived with horses all her life. She loves them, cares for them, lives in a world where they are ridden with consummate skill. Dickens' point is that true knowledge comes from experience and relationship, not from fact and system. The influential Cambridge University literary critic Dr F. R. Leavis at one time admired *Hard Times* above all Dickens' other novels because it starkly dramatized the division between vitality – as embodied by the circus people – and the deadening of the human spirit effected by Gradgrind's educational theory that only facts matter. Gradgrind's academy sought to extirpate children's capacity for wonder, for poetry and imaginary play, in order to prepare them to become factory hands, mechanical cogs in the wheel of Victorian capitalist production. Conversely, the aim of literature teachers in the Leavisite tradition was to create beings of strong feeling and humane understanding. English was often taught with messianic zeal: the study of literature was to be a life-changing and, potentially, a society-changing experience.

A Leavisite – and perhaps a Dickensian – answer to the question 'what is English Literature?' might therefore be 'you know it when you experience it'. Literature means the books that you live with and love, those that embody *life*. An alternative approach, equally contrary to the spirit of Mr Gradgrind, would be to define literature as those books that seem positively to invite the performance of amazing tricks of interpretation, analogous to the riding stunts of the circus people. Literary texts are those in which language is used most cleverly, those that respond to a diversity of readings.

If literature is to be experienced instinctively, or if the *literary* is another word for the *playful*, then to *define* 'English Literature', to reduce it to a set of facts, might be to destroy its peculiar pleasure in an act of unimaginative Gradgrindery. 'We murder to dissect', William Wordsworth once wrote: might the very process of placing a literary work in its generic or historical context be akin to taking a living organism, killing it, and laying it on the laboratory table, then setting about it with a scalpel? This is a common feeling among book lovers when they first encounter critical analysis and literary history, let alone literary theory. They perhaps forget that a work of literature is not a living organism: it is the product of a writer's craft. At the very least, an understanding of the tools of the writer's trade and the journey by which a literary work comes into being should increase rather than diminish the pleasure we take from the finished product.

24

A good English teacher's response to the cry 'we murder to dissect' might go along the following lines: 'If you are a biker, your pleasure in riding at a hundred miles an hour along the motorway will not be diminished – it might positively be enhanced – if you also learn to strip down your bike, work out how it is constructed, tinker with its parts and put it back together again. At the very least, your mechanical expertise will give you good material for conversations with your fellow bikers – and being part of a *community* of bikers, with a shared body of knowledge, customs and traditions, will give you added pleasure.'

Something very similar can be said of the study of English Literature. It can add many extra layers to the pleasure of reading and especially of re-reading; it also makes you part of a literary community. This indeed is also one of the primary pleasures of writing. Writing is among the most solitary of occupations, yet in their minds writers are rarely alone: they share the company of the writers they admire. For John Keats, afflicted with tuberculosis and acutely conscious of his own mortality, it was a comfort to think that he would be, as he put it in a letter, 'among the English poets' after his death.

A dialogue with the dead

Writers nearly always become writers because they are passionate readers. The works of literature that they make their own help to shape the new works they create – usually through a mixture of conscious imitation, unconscious absorption, and active resistance or counter-reaction. The most famous statement of the relationship between literary 'tradition' and the 'individual talent' of a new author remains that of the poet and critic T. S. Eliot:

> No poet, no artist of any art, has his complete meaning alone. His significance, his appreciation, is the appreciation of his relation to the dead poets and artists. You cannot value him alone; you must set him, for contrast and comparison, among the dead. I mean this as a

principle of æsthetic, not merely historical, criticism.... what happens when a new work of art is created is something that happens simultaneously to all the works of art which preceded it. The existing monuments form an ideal order among themselves, which is modified by the introduction of the new (the really new) work of art among them.... the past [is] altered by the present as much as the present is directed by the past.

('Tradition and the Individual Talent', 1919)

The implied politics of Eliot's deference to 'order' and 'tradition' have been subjected to troubled scrutiny, but the idea that the new – the really new – alters our perception of the old is an enduring and irrefutable aesthetic principle. The creation of the literature of the future is dependent on a dialogue with the literature of the past.

A dialogue? How can writers in the past *answer back* to the present? Well, that is exactly what the act of thoughtful and imaginative reading allows them to do. That is why art is one of the traditional ways of defeating death. When an actor speaks a line from Shakespeare or when you attune yourself to the written voice of Jane Austen, a man who died four hundred years ago or a woman who died two hundred years ago return to life, as if by magic. For this reason, elegies on the deaths of poets are usually less sorrowful than those on the deaths of, say, children or the massed victims of war.

Thus W. H. Auden 'In Memory of W. B. Yeats' (1939). At the moment of the poet's death, 'The current of his feeling failed: he became his admirers'. Auden imagines a poet as a person of high-voltage sensibility. When death switches off the electricity, the current is transferred to the poet's readers. The metaphor itself is then switched to a variation on the idea of scattering a dead person's ashes:

> Now he is scattered among a hundred cities
> And wholly given over to unfamiliar affections ...
> The words of a dead man
> Are modified in the guts of the living.

As Auden wrote, the body of Yeats lay in France (later he was reburied, as one of his poems asked that he should be, under Ben Bulben, a mountain that he loved in the west of Ireland), but his poems were already living on in many different locations. Once a literary work is published, it belongs to its readers and no longer to its author. There are restrictive legal rights regarding its reproduction, but there is no copyright control over readerly interiorization and interpretation. Yeats often wrote of, and from, familiar affections – a prayer for his daughter, elegies in memory of his friends and those familiars who gave their lives for Ireland – but poetry lives through what a psychoanalyst might call a *transference* whereby its affect is re-enacted by readers who are not familiar with the writer in person. Shakespeare writes a love-sonnet but when you read it to your lover, it is wholly given over to unfamiliar affections – yours and his/hers. The words of a dead man (Shakespeare, Yeats) are modified in the guts of the living (their posthumous readers).

On form and style

Your first answer to the question 'what is literature?' might well be 'literature is novels, poems and plays'. George Eliot, T. S. Eliot, and Shakespeare are literature. Yes, but Jackie Collins is a novelist, 'Jack and Jill went up the hill' is a poem, and the script of last year's action movie is a screenplay. Do we want to call them literature? If the study of literature simply means the study of words, then the answer would have to be 'yes': the bonkbuster novel, the nursery rhyme, and the blockbuster movie are all made of words. The movie is slightly different in that it is made of visual images and performed actions as well as words, but the same may be said of the difference between a stage play by Shakespeare and a novel by George Eliot or a poem by T. S. Eliot. The nursery rhyme is also slightly different in that we don't know who wrote it and its transmission down the ages has more often been from memory and repetition than text and publication – it is part of what we call the *oral tradition*. But then all longstanding national literatures have their origins in oral tradition.

In the 21st century, the study of 'English' sometimes means the study of words in the English language. The object of the discipline may well be to explore the significance, the *signifying potential*, of popular romantic fiction, nursery rhymes, television soap opera, and the language of advertising. You can learn something about cultural history by comparing and contrasting the words on the labels of cans of baked beans manufactured in the 1950s, 1980s, and 2010s. This sort of analysis has indeed been going on since the 1950s, when the French semiotician (theorist of signs) Roland Barthes published a revelatory book called *Mythologies* (1957), in which he explored the cultural meaning of everything from all-in wrestling to soap powders with the rigour and attention that French intellectuals had previously reserved for the tragedies of Jean Racine and the novels of Gustave Flaubert. Few people, however, would want to claim that the label on a can of baked beans is *literature*. Better names for the disciplines inaugurated by Barthes and his followers are *semiotics* and *cultural studies*. You will find Very Short Introductions to them elsewhere – though there is nothing to stop you applying some of their modes of analysis to the texts that are traditionally called literature.

If metrical form is sufficient to create a piece of poetic literature, then 'Jack and Jill went up the hill' must be admitted to the party along with Shakespeare. Since all young children enjoy rhymes and all cultures have songs and stories in metrical form, this admission is no bad thing. I did not, however, begin this book by saying that your first encounter with English Literature came when your mother dandled you on her knee and sang a nursery rhyme. The word 'literature' comes from the Latin for *letters*, which are written things. The definition from which I want to begin is one in which literature means something that is *written* and that therefore has a writer. By this account, Western *literature* began not when the stories of the Trojan War and

Odysseus' return home to Greece were transmitted orally, but when a scribe wrote those stories on a papyrus roll and ascribed them to an author: *Homer's Iliad* and *Homer's Odyssey*. After reading Homer for a while, even in translation, you feel that you are hearing a very distinctive voice. Yes, there are the repeated formulae derived from the oral tradition ('the wine-dark sea'), but the poem has a structure and a tone that make us believe we are in touch with an authorial consciousness, that there is a pilot steering us on the journey.

The idea of literature implies the idea of an author. But is the presence of an author sufficient to create literature? Must the authors of the generic romance fiction that may be bought in supermarkets be granted a place at the table beside Jane Austen? The answer to this question will depend upon how much time you have. Hundreds of popular romantic novels were published in the lifetime of Jane Austen. To read a few of them will give you some valuable insights into what consumers of fiction wanted in the early 19th century and how a complex artist such as Austen deployed but also transcended the conventions of romantic fiction. It is unlikely, however, that you will gain huge rewards from serial re-reading of these works, as you will from reading Austen 'again and again'.

Rather than saying 'Mills and Boon novels are not literature', it might be better to say 'Jane Austen is good literature but Mills and Boon is bad literature'. Jane Austen wrote tautly constructed sentences, created complicated characters, and wove ingenious plots. Mills and Boon authors write corny sentences, create two-dimensional characters, and rattle through formulaic plots. This distinction may also allow one to introduce the category that George Orwell called 'good bad' literature, among which he included a variety of memorable but sentimental poems and 'escapist' but well-written novels in such genres as romance, thriller, whodunnit, science fiction, and horror story – he considered Bram Stoker's *Dracula* (1897) and Sir Arthur Conan

Doyle's Sherlock Holmes stories (1887–1927) to be very good bad literature.

The figure of Orwell also serves as a reminder that it will not do to define literature as novels, poems, and plays. It surely cannot be the case that Orwell was writing literature when he worked in the form of the novel, as in *Coming Up for Air* (1939), *Animal Farm* (1945), and *Nineteen Eighty-Four* (1949), but non-literature when he worked in the form of memoir and reportage, as in *Down and Out in Paris and London* (1933), *The Road to Wigan Pier* (1937), and *Homage to Catalonia* (1938). Fiction is often based on fact, and factual writing may use as many literary techniques as fictional. And be as well written. What makes Orwell Orwell is not his choice of literary *form*, but the distinctiveness of his literary *style* and *voice*.

Literary criticism has traditionally involved judging pieces of writing on the basis not of *the things said* but of *the way in which they are said*. It is by no means impossible for a scientific treatise, a theological or political tract, a law report, a newspaper article, even an instruction manual, to be written with admirable literary style. Thomas Hobbes's *Leviathan, or the Matter, Form and Power of a Commonwealth Ecclesiastical and Civil* (1651) and Charles Darwin's *The Origin of Species* (1859) can be read with immense pleasure for the sake of their style. Conversely, the over-elaborate style of some literary works may be a positive impediment to pleasure. Judgements regarding style are always subjective. Some people believe that the Russian-born Vladimir Nabokov was the most stylish English-language novelist of the 20th century, while others find his style too clever by half.

The analysis of local stylistic effects is a major component of the literary study of written texts, but the really interesting move comes with the identification of authorial voice. *Literary* authors do more than take care over their choice of words, the shape of their sentences, and the arc of their argument or narrative. They create a written voice that has a distinctive character. 'One may as well begin with Helen's letters to her sister'. The opening of *Howards End* (1910) has the immediate imprint of E. M. Forster's voice: diffident, understated, wry, acutely conscious of the muddles and awkwardness and difficulty we humans – or would Forster have said 'we English'? – have in connecting with each other. The working title of T. S. Eliot's stylistic cornucopia *The Waste Land* (1922) was 'He do the police in different voices'. The art of the very greatest writers is to animate many different voices with equal conviction, but always to leave the imprint of their own distinctive voice. 'Literature expresses, not objective truth, as it is called, but subjective', wrote Cardinal Newman in *The Idea of a University* (Part 2, 1858), 'not things, but thoughts... Literature is the personal use or exercise of language... style is a thinking out into language.'

The literature of power

Dr Johnson's *Dictionary of the English Language* (1755) defined 'literature' as 'Learning; skill in letters'. When Isaac D'Israeli began putting together a compilation called *Curiosities of Literature* in 1791, what he meant by his title was 'a collection of curious lore'. A random sampling of adjacent subjects among his curiosities does not immediately reveal a unifying 'literary' connection – 'Feudal Customs', 'Joan of Arc', 'Gaming', 'Metempsychosis', 'Spanish Etiquette'. Originally, then, the word 'literature' applied to the entire realm of what was known as 'polite letters'. It embraced works of moral and natural philosophy, history, geography, philology, and much more.

By the time the *Oxford English Dictionary* was compiled at the end of the 19th century, a new and more restricted sense of the word had emerged: 'writing which has claim to consideration on the ground of beauty of form or emotional effect'. The emergence of this particularized category of writing was tied to a new term, the *aesthetic*, which was first developed in Germany in the 18th century

and which Samuel Taylor Coleridge did more than anyone else
to bring into currency in England. Aesthetics was the art of judging
the beautiful.

Pioneer of aesthetic criticism that Coleridge was, his own usage of
the term 'literature' remained the traditional one. In his
Biographia Literaria: Sketches of My Literary Life and Opinions
(1817), he refers to 'polite literature' in the manner of the
18th-century term 'polite letters'. The eleventh chapter of the
Biographia addresses the question of whether it is possible to make
a profession – or a trade – out of authorship. Here Coleridge's
exemplars of 'weighty performances in literature' are Cicero
(ancient Roman politician, moralist, and rhetorician), Xenophon
(ancient Greek historian and biographer), Sir Thomas More
(historian, theologian, politician, and author of *Utopia*, a treatise/
satire/fantasy on the nature of an ideal society), Sir Francis Bacon
(politician, historian, essayist, theorist of law, author of treatises on
society, on knowledge, on myth, pioneer of empirical method),
Richard Baxter (Puritan theologian and autobiographer), Erasmus
Darwin (versifier of scientific, especially botanical and zoological,
knowledge), and William Roscoe (biographer, poet, legal theorist,
and author of powerful anti-slavery tracts). The major writings of
all these authors are all historically, morally, scientifically, or
politically purposeful rather than in the domain of the aesthetic, of
literature considered as one of the 'fine arts'.

It was in a series of essays published in *The London Magazine*, a
forum for much of the best new writing of the early 1820s, that
Thomas De Quincey ('the English opium-eater') made a radical
new move. He defined literature by *opposing* it to the general body
of written knowledge. Partly as a way of coping with the sheer
volume of literature in the original broad sense of the word,
De Quincey created a new and much more refined definition:

> The word *literature* is a perpetual source of confusion, because it is
> used in two senses, and those senses liable to be confounded with

each other. In a philosophical use of the word, Literature is the
direct and adequate antithesis of Books of Knowledge. But, in a
popular use, it is a mere term of convenience for expressing
inclusively the total books of a language.

('Letters to a Young Man whose Education has been Neglected',
London Magazine, 1823)

The popular sense embraces the hundreds of thousands of volumes
that made De Quincey melancholy whenever he entered a great
library and realized what a small proportion of them he would ever
have time to read. In this sense, literature includes 'a dictionary,
a grammar, a spelling-book, an almanac, a pharmacopoeia, a
Parliamentary report, a system of farriery, a treatise on billiards,
the Court Calendar, etc.' What De Quincey calls the 'philosophical
sense', on the other hand, must exclude all these, and even 'books of
much higher pretensions' such as histories and travel narratives;
'all books', in fact, 'in which the matter to be communicated is
paramount to the manner or form of its communication'.
'Literature', then, is writing which must be judged according to the
criterion of significant form, that is to say, on the basis of aesthetic
more than cognitive effect.

In an inspired coinage, De Quincey lumped 'Books of Knowledge'
together as 'anti-literature'. What, then, is the antithesis to
Knowledge, which will define what Literature is books of? One
possible answer would have been to say of literature what had often
been said of *poetry*. There was an old argument that whereas the
function of writing in general is the communication of truth, the
immediate end of poetry is the communication of pleasure. The
art of poetry, according to Horace in ancient Rome, is to instruct
and to please. Dr Johnson was following this classical precept
when he said that the end of writing is to instruct whereas the
end of poetry is to instruct by pleasing. For De Quincey, however,
pleasure is a 'vulgar antithesis' to knowledge. Pleasure is akin to
idle amusement, and it is not for this that we read *Paradise Lost*.
'The true antithesis to knowledge, in this case, is not *pleasure*, but

power. All that is literature seeks to communicate power; all that is not literature, to communicate knowledge.'

This is De Quincey's decisive formulation. Literature makes its readers 'feel vividly, and with a vital consciousness, emotions which ordinary life rarely or never supplies occasions for exciting, and which had previously lain unawakened, and hardly within the dawn of consciousness'. De Quincey's first example of the power of literature is Shakespeare's King Lear in the storm: on confronting the scene, 'I am thus suddenly startled into a feeling of the infinity of the world within me'. His second example develops the idea of literature as the opposite of science. Whereas a writer in pursuit of knowledge such as the philosopher Leibniz relies on mathematical learning in order to write about space, the titanic shapes of Milton in *Paradise Lost* transform space from a geometric concept into a living power: 'from being a thing to inscribe with diagrams, it has become under his hands a vital agent on the human mind'.

'The proper sense of the word literature', wrote De Quincey in the fourth of his 'Letters to a Young Man', is 'a body of creative art'. The use of the word 'creative' in relation to the imagination was again extremely new in the early 19th century. De Quincey was probably thinking of the elevated claim that opens Wordsworth's sonnet to the painter Benjamin Robert Haydon, 'High is our calling, Friend! – Creative Art'. Developing Wordsworth's and Coleridge's faith in the high calling of the poet, De Quincey came to define literature specifically as 'a body of creative art'. He was the first to define it thus, and the definition has been enormously influential: he was, if you will, the inventor of Literature with a capital L.

Canon and repertoire

One of the few uncontestable statements about English Literature is that it is an examination subject which can be taken for the General Certificate of Secondary Education, at both Ordinary and

Advanced levels, in the state-approved school curriculum in Britain. It is also the name of a degree course in many universities in a number of countries around the world. A theoretically unsophisticated but potentially quite useful answer to the question 'what is English Literature?' might accordingly be 'English Literature is the content prescribed for study in school and university courses called English Literature'. If it's on a syllabus somewhere, it qualifies as literature. Otherwise it doesn't. This is a move that shifts the definition from production – where or by whom or in what language the work was written, whether or not it was composed with style, care, and distinctive voice – to consumption. Is it sold with the apparatus of a textbook, that is to say, replete with critical introduction, explanatory notes, account of textual issues, bibliography of scholarly studies? Is it marketed as a Penguin Classic or a World's Classic? Is it deemed worthy of close analysis in the classroom and dissection under exam conditions? Can advanced students of English Literature get a PhD by writing about it?

A word that is sometimes used for the books that are on a syllabus somewhere is 'the canon'. English Literature is sometimes said to be synonymous with the canon. Perhaps one should imagine a kind of virtual conference of every Professor of English Literature in the world, in which they act as a global examination board which, after hours (more realistically years) of debate, prescribes the list of texts for study. These, they have agreed, are the books that have earned the capital L at the beginning of Literature.

The fallacy in this fantasy becomes apparent when we reflect on the origin of the word 'canon'. In AD 393, the Synod of Hippo, under the authority of St Augustine, approved the canon of books that made up the New Testament. All other gospels and epistles were henceforth deemed apocryphal or non-canonical. The New Testament canon was thus closed, though during the Reformation in the 16th century Martin Luther tried to remove the books of Hebrews, James, Jude, and Revelation. The Old Testament canon was unstable for longer, but in 1546 it was dogmatically articulated (for the Roman Catholic Church) by the Council of Trent. The Church of England's – slightly different – canon was fixed seventeen years later among the Thirty-Nine Articles of Anglican faith.

The problem for our putative virtual conference of Professors of English is not only that they do not have the authority of the Council of Trent, but also that the body of English Literature does not purport to offer divine revelation – nor does it belong solely to the distant past, as is the case with the biblical canon. New works with the *potential* to achieve subsequent 'canonical' status are published every day. Old works go out of print, out of fashion. They drop out of the syllabus. Other old works, long neglected, come into new favour. There was a time when the plays of Beaumont and Fletcher were staged more frequently than those of Shakespeare. The hand-crafted prophetic books of William Blake found no more than a handful of readers in his lifetime but are now the font of a substantial scholarly industry. Dozens of exquisite poems by John Clare were published for the first time over a hundred years after his death. The 'canon' of 17th- and 18th-century English Literature was for a lengthy period assumed to consist almost entirely of works by men, but in the late 20th century numerous admirable novels, plays, and poems by women were brought back into print. The history of theological canon formation has no equivalent for these extreme and rapid vicissitudes. The turnover of books in the library of English Literature is such that the idea of a literary canon, with its image of authority and stability, is one that must be treated with caution.

The relative popularity on the London stage of Beaumont and Fletcher on the one hand, Shakespeare on the other (more Beaumont and Fletcher in the 1660s, complete Shakespearean domination with effect from the 1730s), gives us a more helpful word than 'canon', namely *repertoire*. A play or an opera becomes a classic when it endures in the repertoire for a long time. Some hardy perennials drop away over time, while ingenious stage directors revive lost gems.

In the 18th century, various publishers attempted to stabilize the repertoire by publishing multi-volume editions of 'The English Poets'. Dr Johnson's *Lives of the Poets* were commissioned as introductions to one such collection. But then in the early 19th century, there were new collections, introducing more recent poets and casting aside many of the older ones. The repertoire of English Literature evolves, shaped ultimately by market forces – whether a work speaks strongly enough to a later age to win an audience and sell books for publishers.

Sophisticated critical opinion plays a significant but by no means absolute role in this process. Consider the internal repertoire of Shakespeare's plays. In 1819, an article in *Blackwood's Edinburgh Magazine* asserted that Shakespeare's four greatest tragedies were *Hamlet, King Lear, Macbeth*, and *Othello*. In 1904, the influential critic A. C. Bradley reinforced this opinion by devoting his published lectures *Shakespearean Tragedy* to these plays, calling them the 'big four'. For two hundred years, they have been assured a place in the theatrical repertoire and on the academic syllabus, whilst, say, *Timon of Athens* and *Titus Andronicus* have not. But then *Romeo and Juliet* has, over the same period, been the most frequently staged of all Shakespeare's plays, despite the fact that Bradley and many other academic analysts have been rather sniffy about it (teenagers in love not a proper subject for mature tragedy, don't you know?). Meanwhile, to the astonishment of most Shakespearean scholars born before the year 1950, *Titus Andronicus* has recently become one of the plays most enjoyed and admired by students. The academic and the stage repertoire have proceeded in tandem: in both the study and the theatre, *Titus* is now central whereas *Timon* remains marginal.

The repertoire of English Literature has been shaped not only by critics and opinion-formers, by publishing houses and circulating libraries, by copyright laws and examination boards, but also by writers themselves. Those processes of translation, imitation, absorption, and reaction recycle and thus revivify the literature of the past. This, again, is literature's dialogue with the dead, Eliot's individual talent modifying the tradition.

The shadows of futurity

Poets, wrote P. B. Shelley, are 'the hierophants of an unapprehended inspiration, the mirrors of the gigantic shadows which futurity casts upon the present' ('A Defence of Poetry', 1821). If this were not the case, the literature of the past would be no more than a collection of historical documents. Of course, the literature of the past *is* a collection of historical documents, worthy of historical study and readily illuminated by the application of historical method. But contained within the idea of Literature in De Quincey's special sense is a faith in the capacity of human beings not to be entirely bound by history, confined by time and circumstance.

The paradox of Literature is the simultaneous presence and absence of the author. On the one hand, the work is marked by the author's unique identity, which I have called *written voice*. On the other hand, as Auden has it, the author becomes his (or her) admirers. 'Poetry makes nothing happen', Auden wrote in that same elegy on the death of Yeats. And yet, a few lines later, 'it survives, / A way of happening, a mouth'.

Literature is a mouth: it is the form of art that uses words as opposed to images (the visual arts) or music. But great literature shares some essential characteristics with great artworks in other media. Had Albert Einstein not worked out the equation $E = mc^2$, someone else would have done so a few years later. If there had been no Charles Darwin, Alfred Wallace would have been credited with the discovery that evolution functions through natural selection according to fitness to environment. But if Milton had not written *Paradise Lost*, no one else would have done. And if there had been no Beethoven, the whole history of Western music would have been different.

Among the chief rules of science are verifiability and replicability. Other researchers should be able to check your evidence and replicate your results when they perform your experiment themselves. Among the chief rules of art are non-verifiability and non-replicability. Though works of art are usually intended to tell us something about how the world is, they do not have to be verifiable. They are not reliant upon 'evidence'. Indeed, one way of describing them is precisely as 'second' or 'other' or, as we might now say, 'virtual' worlds. And though works of art must be mechanically *reproduced* in order to have any lasting effect, they cannot be *replicated*. This is the serious point behind the joke in Jorge Luis Borges' story 'Pierre Menard, the author of the *Quixote*' (1941). Menard is a fictional 20th-century French writer who immerses himself deeply in the 17th-century world of Miguel de Cervantes' *Don Quixote* in order not merely to translate the work but to recreate it. He eventually does so, by translating it word for word into Cervantes' original 17th-century Spanish. Borges thus has it both ways: on the one hand, Menard's reproduction serves only to demonstrate the uniqueness of Cervantes' work (asked what he *meant* by one of his piano sonatas, the composer Robert Schumann is alleged to have played it again), but on the other hand, the re-creation of the work in a different cultural context changes its meaning (things that were not archaic in Cervantes have become archaisms in Menard).

All literature is influenced by social and historical context – what human activity is not? – but a distinguishing characteristic of an enduring literary work is precisely its capacity to *resist* the context of its moment of production, maybe even to resist the knowledge and the intentions of its author. John Keats remarked in a letter, 'Things which I do half at random are afterwards confirmed by my judgment in a dozen features of propriety'. That is to say, artists are not fully in control of the processes whereby their creations come into being. For Keats, this is the magical alchemy of art. From the writer's point of view, it is the literary work itself that does the controlling, not, as some modern critics would have it, the historical or ideological context of the moment of production.

A truly literary work is one that takes on a life of its own, like Pygmalion's statue in the Greek myth. Keats's 'Ode on a Grecian Urn' is a meditation on this idea. In some mysterious sense, the work of art creates its own shape and in so doing makes possible its own future after it has left the hands of the artist. 'That which is creative must create itself' – Keats again. If only metaphorically, the great work of art *is* after all a living organism. Its greatness is defined by its capacity to evolve, as successful living organisms do, through adaptation to new cultural environments. It survives to meet the futurity whose shadow is cast upon its origin.

Chapter 3
When it began

The Irish Question

In 1969, the Northern Irish poet Seamus Heaney bought himself a
Christmas present: a book called *The Bog People* by P. V. Glob. It
told of the discovery of prehistoric human bodies preserved
beneath the peat bogs of Denmark. Heaney had been brought up
on a farm and felt a deep bond with the life of the soil; the
signature poem in his first collection, *Death of a Naturalist* (1966),
was called 'Digging'. He became fascinated by the image of bog
people: their belonging in the land, their simultaneous mortality
(the bodies bore the marks of violent death) and immortality (their
retention of human form over thousands of years). He wrote a
group of poems inspired by them. In 'Punishment', he drew an
analogy between the corpse of a ritually sacrificed bog woman and
the treatment of Roman Catholic girls in Belfast who in the
'Troubles' during which he was writing were ritually tarred and
chained to their front porches for dating British soldiers. The
analogy gained force not least from the longstanding English insult
whereby the Irish were called 'bogtrotters'.

As an Irish poet writing in the English language, Heaney was
acutely conscious that his spoken tongue and the literary tradition
into which he was entering belonged to the people who had
conquered the Irish land and oppressed the Irish people. Edmund

Spenser, the 'national' poet in the age of Elizabeth I, served as a government official in Ireland and wrote a political dialogue called *A View of the Present State of Ireland* in which the dominant voice advocates the violent suppression of the rebellious Irish (though the story is more complicated than this – Spenser's animus was directed less against the indigenous Gaelic Irish than the 'old English' who had been in Ireland since the 12th century, an early glimmer of the perennial imperial fear of the colonial settlers going native). Another Heaney poem, 'Act of Union', wittily elides the formal annexation of Ireland with the sexual conquest of an Irish servant girl by another Elizabethan proto-imperial poet, Sir Walter Ralegh.

In 'The Tollund Man', Heaney drives through the country of the bog people:

> Saying the names
> Tollund, Grauballe, Nebelgard,
> Watching the pointing hands
> Of country people,
> Not knowing their tongue.
> Out here in Jutland
> In the old man-killing parishes
> I will feel lost,
> Unhappy and at home.

> (*Wintering Out*, 1972)

He is in Jutland, where the Anglo-Saxons had come from: the original home of the race that would drive out the Celts, his own people. He is 'lost' but also 'at home'. This may be the perpetual condition of the poet, but in 1969 a dual sense of belonging and not belonging was particularly acute for a thoughtful Northern Irish Catholic. Heaney is a man of words, fascinated by the sounds of the names that have been given to the bog people, as he is by the old Irish names of his own place. But he does not write in Gaelic. The 'pointing hands' thus become those of his own 'country people', admonishing him for not knowing his native tongue. A few years later, Heaney's friend Brian Friel wrote an immensely powerful play about the remapping of Irish places with new British names (*Translations*, 1980). In the poems collected in *North* (1975), we witness Heaney progging at his own anxiety that by writing in English he may have participated in a betrayal.

At some level, he is wondering whether one of the bog men could have been a poet, a guardian of the land and language, a vessel for the preservation of the stories of a tribe. For that was the original role of poets, as Spenser himself recognized, with a touch of envy, in *A View of the Present State of Ireland*:

> There is amongst the Irish a certain kind of people called Bards, which are to them instead of poets, whose profession is to set forth the praises or dispraises of men in their poems or rhymes, the which are had in so high regard and estimation amongst them, that none dare displease them.

Celts

There is an ancient history behind all this, a fact that is scandalous to the Anglocentric version of literary history: before the English there were the Celts. The poems of the Celts, not those of the late-coming Anglo-Saxon invaders, were the native equivalent of the Homeric corpus on which ancient Greek culture was built. A mythologized version of the Celtic bard is a key figure in the history of literature in these islands. The harp that accompanied the song of the bard has been a potent and enduring symbol, especially in Wales and Ireland. But since Celtic culture was oral, the poems of the bards were not written down for many centuries.

'"And this also," said Marlow suddenly, "has been one of the dark places of the earth"' (Joseph Conrad, *Heart of Darkness*, 1902). Ironically, in so far as Britain would one day become an empire that modelled itself on ancient Rome, the earliest written text regarding Britannia was written not by a native but by the leader of a colonial expeditionary force. Julius Caesar, in the fifth book of his *Gallic Wars*, created an enduring image of the inhabitants of the triangular island off the north coast of Gaul: 'All the Britons, indeed, dye themselves with wood, which occasions a bluish colour, and thereby have a more terrible appearance in fight. They wear their hair long, and have every part of their body shaved except their head and upper lip.' Caesar failed to establish a colony in Britannia, though he did extract an agreement that tribute money would be paid to Rome. Aulus Plautius, leading an invasion force nearly a century later, in AD 43, was more successful. Roads, villas, baths, a wall to keep out the Picts of the north, and eventually Christianity would arrive in his wake. British resistance to the Roman invader would become part of the national myth in later centuries. During the reign of King James I of England, who was also King James VI of Scotland and who had hopes of uniting his two kingdoms to create a new 'Britain', Celtic resistance to Roman imperialism provided Shakespeare with the plot of his *Cymbeline* (c. 1610) and John Fletcher with his *Bonduca* (c. 1613, an alternative spelling of Boudicca or Boadicea).

Crucially, though, the Romans never invaded Ireland. This meant that the bardic tradition of the Celts was still alive when St Patrick converted Ireland to Christianity in the 5th century. Literate monks began to write down and preserve the stories of the native culture – sequences of epic poetry such as the 'Ulster' cycle, narrating the exploits of Cú Chulainn, and the 'Finn' or 'Fenian' cycle, telling of Finn or Fionn, foremost among the elite warriors of the Irish High King.

Neither the Romans, nor the next wave of invaders, the Anglo-Saxons, penetrated into Scotland or the depths of Wales. Celtic stories accordingly survived in these lands too. Again, though, they were not written down for hundreds of years. The Welsh *Mabinogion*, meaning 'instructions for young bards', tells of Pwyll, prince of Dyved, and Branwen, daughter of Llyr. The collection appears in a manuscript known as the 'Red Book of Hergest', which belongs to the late 14th century. In Scotland, stories were handed down regarding the exploits of Oisin, legendary 3rd-century warrior and bard, son of Finn (Fingal).

The translation – or, more often, the free adaptation and reinvention – of these foundational epics into the English language has been an important feature of various Celtic revivals. In 1760, after the failure of the Jacobite political enterprise to return the Stuart kings to the throne, a Scotsman called James Macpherson tried launching a cultural revolution instead. He published *Fragments of Ancient Poetry collected in the Highlands of Scotland, and translated from the Gaelic or Erse language*. Spurred by the success of this enterprise, he followed it up two years later with *Fingal, an Ancient Epic Poem in Six Books*, and the year after that with an eight-book epic called *Temora*, purportedly the work of Ossian (Oisin) himself:

> Is the wind on the shield of Fingal? Or is the voice of past times in my hall? ... Four times has autumn returned with its winds, and raised the seas of Togorma, since thou hast been in the roar of battles, and Bragéla distant far!

('The Death of Cuthullin')

Could Macpherson have recovered the British equivalent of Homer? Many people thought so, but others were suspicious – notably, Dr Samuel Johnson, an Englishman with a low opinion of Scottish culture. 'But Doctor Johnson,' he was asked, 'do you really believe that any man today could write such poetry?' 'Yes,' he replied, 'Many men. Many women. And many children.' Macpherson was called upon to produce his originals and was obliged to fabricate them. In very British fashion, a committee of inquiry was established. It concluded, and modern scholarship has largely endorsed its findings, that Macpherson had (very) liberally edited a body of traditional Gaelic ballads and inserted swathes of his own writing. Though the Ossian affair hardly served the

Jacobite cause, the romantic sublimity of the poems' language helped to shift English poetry away from the neoclassical mode that had dominated for much of the 18th century. William Blake attempted to create an entirely new kind of 'radical British' epic in *Milton* and *Jerusalem* by rejecting Greco-Latin models and seeking to combine the style of Ossian with that of the prophetic books of the Hebrew Bible.

A century later, the Celtic revival in Ireland played a major part in the emergence of a cultural nationalism forged in resistance to British rule. Leading figures in this movement included members of the old Anglo-Irish protestant ascendancy such as Lady Gregory, who translated and adapted many stories about the legendary hero Cuchulain, and William Butler Yeats, who published *Fairy and Folk Tales of the Irish Peasantry* (1888), *The Wanderings of Oisin and Other Poems* (1889), and *The Celtic Twilight* (1893). In 1899, his *The Countess Cathleen* was acted at the Irish Literary Theatre, which he and Lady Gregory had founded. In December 1904, the 'national' Abbey Theatre opened its doors in Dublin with a triple bill of Yeats's *On Baile's Strand* (a play about Cuchulain) and *Cathleen Ní Houlihan*, together with Lady Gregory's *Spreading the News*, a comedy that satirized the English ruling class via the character of a pompous Magistrate. On the second night, one of the Yeats plays was replaced by *In the Shadow of the Glen* by J. M. Synge, another dramatist from a well-to-do protestant background who converted to Irish cultural nationalism and made his work out of the stories of the folk – in his case, those of the Aran Islands.

In a poem in memory of Major Robert Gregory, Lady Gregory's son, Yeats wrote that Synge had found his inspiration 'In a most desolate stony place', that he came 'Towards nightfall upon a race / Passionate and simple like his heart'. The Celtic revivals were bound up not only with politics and nationalism, but also with a poetic desire to return to peasant simplicity and strong feeling while grounding the religious sense in locality and landscape.

Anglo-Saxons

When the Anglo-Saxons arrived in wave upon wave from Jutland, Angeln, Saxony, and Frisia, they brought their own tales of legendary heroes. Again, these were only written down much later. The most famous of their stories is *Beowulf*. There is a lively scholarly debate about the date of its composition (8th century or much later?). The only surviving manuscript belongs to the late 10th or 11th century; it was recovered in the 16th. *Beowulf* embodies the poetry of Old English at its most forceful, but since it was unknown for so long and was set in Scandinavia, it exercised no influence on English literature until the 19th century, when it was translated into modern English. In more recent times, it has been studied in universities and translated many times, not least by Heaney, for whom it provided an opportunity to make peace with his Anglo-Saxon masters after the reconciliation of the 1999 Good Friday agreement. He was drawn especially to the poem's earthbound language and its alliterative energy ('Sinews split / and the bone-lappings burst').

'Ossian' was in large measure fabricated and the author of *Beowulf* is unknown. Who, then, was the first English poet who can be named, as Homer can be named as the founding father who began the journey from the unknown singers of oral tradition to the revered authors of 'literature'?

In Anglo-Saxon England, writing was predominantly the preserve of monks. Literacy belonged to the clerks, which is to say the clerics. The most potent narrative of the origin of English Literature is accordingly to be found in a clerical text. Written in Latin, it was the Venerable Bede's *Historia ecclesiastica gentis Anglorum* ('Ecclesiastical History of the English People', believed to have been completed in AD 731), a nascent national history in which the main focus is on the conflict between Roman and Celtic Christianity.

According to Bede, some time in the late 7th century, when St Hild was abbot of Streanæshalch (Whitby) on the north-east coast of England, there lived a man called Cædmon who composed 'godly and religious songs'. He studied the Scriptures and their interpreters, turning passages of the Testaments 'into extremely delightful and moving poetry, in English, which was his own tongue'. All that survives of his creations is a single fragment. A visitor came to Cædmon in a dream and told him that he must sing in praise of God the Creator. This is what he sang:

Nu we sculon herigean   heonfonrices Weard,
Now we should praise the heaven-kingdom's guardian,
Meotodes meahte   ond his modgeþanc,
the measurer's might and his mind-conception,
weorc Wuldorfæder,   swa he wundra gehwæs,
work of the glorious father, as he each wonder,
ece Drihten,   or onstealde.
eternal Lord, instilled at the origin.
He ærest sceop   eorðan bearnum
He first created for earth's sons
heofon to hrofe,   halig Scyppend.
heaven as a roof, holy creator;
þa middangeard   monncynnes Weard,
then, middle-earth, mankind's guardian,
ece Drihten,   æfter teode
eternal Lord, afterward made
firum foldan,   Frea ælmihtig.
the earth for men, father almighty.

From its very beginning in these lines, English poetry has resonated with the language of praise and of wonder; writers have taken it upon themselves to be the guardians of 'middangeard', 'middle earth'. The poet's creative spark emulates God's: there is a golden thread linking Cædmon to Samuel Taylor Coleridge's definition, over a thousand years later, of the poetic imagination as a repetition in the finite mind of the eternal act of creation in the infinite 'I am'.

In Cædmon's time, England was still divided into several kingdoms. The invention of English poetry preceded the formation of the English nation. So when did a *national* literature emerge?

Alfred, King of Wessex from 871 to 899, had a new conception of his royal role. He aspired to excellence 'both in warfare and in wisdom'. He considered it his duty not only to preserve his kingdom from the Viking hordes, but also to establish his court as a cultural centre and to oversee the creation of a vernacular literary culture. He wrote, or perhaps commissioned, translations from the Bible (a prose version of the first fifty Psalms), from Christian theological and pragmatic texts (Augustine's *Soliloquies* and Gregory's *Pastoral Care*), and from Roman neo-Stoic philosophy (Boethius' *Consolation of Philosophy*, which would be translated again by Chaucer many centuries later). 'King Alfred was the translator of this book', began the preface to his Boethius, 'he turned it from Latin into English, as it now stands before you. Sometimes he translated word for word, sometimes sense for sense, so as to render it as clearly and intelligibly as he could, given the various and multifarious worldly distractions which frequently occupied him either in mind or in body.' In the following millennium, Queen Elizabeth I and King James VI/I would follow in Alfred's footsteps as monarchs who found time for reading, writing, and translation. Translation – which in the 17th century the poet John Dryden would divide into literal 'metaphrase', freer 'paraphrase', and creative 'imitation' – has been a perennial project of English Literature.

Though Alfred was perhaps the first to create a repertoire of literature in the English language, he was not king of all the land. According to a poem in *The Anglo-Saxon Chronicle*, it was in the year 937 that

> Athelstan King,
> Lord among Earls,

Bracelet-bestower and
Baron of Barons,
He with his Brother,
Edmund Atheling,
Gaining a lifelong
Glory in battle,
Slew with the sword-edge
There by Brunanburh,
Brake the shield-wall,
Hew'd the linden-wood,
Hack'd the battle-shield,
Sons of Edward with hammer'd brands.

('The Battle of Brunanburh', translated by Alfred Lord Tennyson, 1876)

In this battle, which took place at a location that is still debated (the leading contender is Bromborough on the Wirral), a Saxon army defeated an alliance of Vikings, Scots, and Irish. Thereafter Athelstan, Alfred's grandson, was the first king of all England. But the cultural identity of his land remained hybrid. Though the Anglo-Saxons were dominant, they jostled with the legacies of native Celts, Norse invaders, and Christian missionaries. When the Normans came in 1066, the picture was complicated further.

After the Norman Conquest

Nowhere is the intersection of different ethnic and linguistic traditions more apparent than in the stories of Britain's mythical founder, Brutus, and its exemplary king, Arthur. Ancient Rome had trumped Greece by proclaiming its mythic origins in the escape of Aeneas from Troy. After the fall of the Roman empire, British chroniclers deployed the same tactic as a means of asserting their own venerable pedigree. The story is first encountered in the 9th-century *Historia Brittonum* of Nennius; it was told most influentially in Geoffrey of Monmouth's 12th-century *Historia Regum Britanniae* ('History of the Kings of Britain'). A Welshman in Oxford at a time when England was ruled by the Normans, Geoffrey sought to trump the Saxons by proclaiming the superior antiquity of the Celts.

In this narrative, the British are given the same origin as the Romans. Brutus, the great-grandson of Aeneas, accidentally kills his father and goes into exile. He meets up with the last remnants of the Trojan race, frees them from the Greeks, and leads them on a voyage to the distant northern island of Albion, which was then uninhabited save for the last few of an old race of giants. They land at Totnes in the West Country and Brutus renames the island after himself. His followers become Britons. Geoffrey then outlines two thousand years of mythic British history. The line of kings inaugurated by Brutus includes many who would be featured in Elizabethan and Jacobean drama, such as Locrine, Gorboduc, Ferrex and Porrex, Lear, and Cymbeline. The *Historia* ends with the death of Arthur, the greatest of these kings, and the prophecy that his line would one day be revived. Cue the Tudor propagandists four centuries later: they pointed to Henry VII's Welsh ancestry as evidence that this new dynasty was made of true Arthurian, and ultimately Brutish/Trojan, stock.

The line of Brutus was a myth, but Geoffrey's narrative drew at various points on true history. Before the Romans renamed it Londinium, Britain's first city took its name from a powerful local tribe, the Trinovantes. Trinovantium could thus be reinterpreted as Troynovantum, new Troy. So Edmund Spenser in the third book of the Elizabethan *Faerie Queene*: 'For noble *Britons* sprong from *Troians* bold, / And *Troynouant* was built of old *Troyes* ashes cold'.

Geoffrey's history was written in Latin prose. It was turned into French verse by Wace, who presented his *Roman de Brut* to Queen Eleanor (wife of Henry II) in 1155. Then around 1215, it was translated into early Middle English by a man called Laȝamon ('lawman'), who wrote in a West Midland dialect that still has the feel of Old English. Laȝamon retained strong elements of the old alliterative verse style and used a surprisingly small number of words of French origin, even when his translation was comparatively literal. He also expanded and improvised upon his material, as when he introduced a prophecy of return after the passing of Arthur:

> Aefne than worden ther com of se wenden
> That was an sceort bat lithen, sceoven mid üthen;
> And two wimmen therinne, wunderliche i-dihte;
> And heo nomen Arthur anan and a-neouste hine vereden
> And softe him a-dun leiden, and forth gunnen hine lithen.
>
> Tha wes hit i-wurthen that Merlin seide whilen,
> That weore unimete care of Arthures forthfare.
> Brüttes i-leveth yete that he bön on live
> And wunnien in Avalun mid fairest alre alven,
> And lokieth ever Brüttes yete whan Arthur cumen lithe.
> Nis naver the mon i-boren of naver nane bürde i-coren
> The cunne of than soothe of Arthure sügen mare.
> But while wes an witeghe, Merlin i-hate;
> He bodede mid worde – his quithes weoren soothe –
> That an Arthur sculde yete cum Anglen to fülste.

Even at these words, there came travelling from the sea a short boat, moving, driven by the waves, and two women in it, wondrously clad; and they took Arthur into it and went in beside him and laid him down gently, and they journeyed away.

Then was fulfilled what Merlin had previously said, that there would be unbounded sorrow at the departure of Arthur. The Britons still believe that he is alive and dwells in Avalon with the fairest of all elves, and the Britons ever look for the time, even yet, when Arthur will come back. Never has the man been born of any chosen woman that can tell more of the truth concerning Arthur. But once there was a wizard called Merlin; he announced by word – his sayings were true – that an Arthur was still to come as an aid to the English.

Whereas Cædmon's hymn sounds like a foreign language, the usage of phrases such as 'two wimmen therinne' in Laȝamon's *Brut* begins to sound like modern English. And in that slide from the British ('Brüttes') to the English ('Anglen'), Laȝamon anticipates one of the prevailing tensions of the national story.

King Arthur would indeed return, but by a circuitous route. In the 12th and 13th centuries, the tales of his knights of the Round Table were developed in the French romance tradition, most notably by Chrétien de Troyes. They were then central to a revival of English alliterative poetry in the 14th century, before receiving their most influential recension in Thomas Malory's 15th-century prose narrative *Morte Darthur*, which brought together French and English sources, along with developments that were Malory's invention. William Caxton's printed text of 1485 assured wider circulation than was achievable within manuscript culture.

In every subsequent century, poets have returned to the matter of Arthur, among them William Warner (*Albion's England*) and Edmund Spenser (*The Faerie Queene*) in the 16th; John Milton in the 17th (he planned an Arthurian epic before settling on the biblical matter of *Paradise Lost*); Lord Tennyson in the 19th (*Idylls of the King*); and Simon Armitage in the 21st (translations of *Sir Gawain and the Green Knight* and *The Alliterative Morte Arthure*). For Armitage, a Yorkshire poet in the mould of Ted Hughes and Tony Harrison, the story of Gawain's perilous journey far away from Camelot to the chapel of the Green Knight exemplifies an anti-metropolitan, grounded, northern English dialect:

> Ouer at þe Holy Hede, til he hade eft bonk
> In þe wyldrenesse of Wyrale; wonde þer bot lyte
> þat auþer God oþer gome wyth goud hert louied....
> Sumwhyle wyth wormez he werrez, and with wolues als,
> Sumwhyle wyth wodwos, þat woned in þe knarrez,
> Boþe wyth bullez and berez, and borez oþerquyle.
>
> (*Sir Gawain and the Green Knight*, fitt 2)

Crossing at Holy Head and coming ashore
in the wilds of the Wirral, whose wayward people
both God and good men have quite given up on....
Here he scraps with serpents and snarling wolves,
here he tangles with wodwos causing trouble in the crags
or with bulls and bears and the odd wild boar.

(translated by Simon Armitage, 2007)

Chaucer versus Langland

Roman versus Briton, Saxon versus Celt, Norman versus Saxon, writing in Latin or French versus writing in English, court versus country, south versus north, received pronunciation versus regional dialect, London versus the provinces: English Literature has been built upon the contest between conqueror and dispossessed, centre and margin, authority and rebellion. Several of these tensions are vividly apparent in the diverging legacies of the two great poets of the late 14th century.

The son of a vintner, Geoffrey Chaucer was born a Londoner. As a young man, he had a period of military service in France, during which he was captured and ransomed. He then gained the patronage of the hugely powerful John of Gaunt; his most notable early poem, *The Boke of the Duchesse* (c. 1368), was dedicated to the memory of Blanche of Lancaster, Gaunt's first wife. Chaucer's wife Philippa was sister to the duke's mistress. With connections such as this, it was easy for Chaucer to gain some rewarding positions at court. A mission to Genoa and Florence on the king's service in the early 1370s was especially important for his poetic development because it gave him the opportunity to discover the riches of Italian literature. It has been suggested – though most scholars discount the possibility – that he may even have met Boccaccio and Petrarch, the pre-eminent authors of the Italian Renaissance. Back in London, he obtained the posts of comptroller of customs and then clerk of the king's works.

2. Geoffrey Chaucer, in the margin of the Ellesmere manuscript of *The Canterbury Tales*, beside the 'Tale of Melibee', which the poet narrates himself

For Chaucer, poetry was an accomplishment and a vehicle for self-display, a means to advancement at court rather than a profession. His poetry benefited his career and vice-versa: his earlier works, coinciding with his French connections, were influenced by French poetry (notably the allegorical love vision of the *Roman de la Rose*), while his middle period, inspired by the Italian journey, was dominated by his version of the Troilus and Cressida story, written in imitation of Boccaccio's treatment of the same subject.

55

Courtly, cosmopolitan, and multi-lingual, Chaucer was a self-consciously modern and, above all, a European poet. His poetry and translations were celebrated among the elite. Even when he turned, late in life, to the *Canterbury Tales*, with their satirical anatomizing of English character types, each representing a different role or 'estate' within the polity, he continued to domesticate continental models and update inherited ones. The idea of multiple narrations within a single overarching structure is derived from Boccaccio's *Decameron*; the Knight's Tale is adapted from another work by Boccaccio; the bawdy Miller's Tale is in the style of French *fabliau*; the Monk's Tale is shaped by the classical notion of tragedy as the fall of great men; the Nun's Priest's Tale is a beast fable in a tradition going back to Aesop; the Wife of Bath is a larger-than-life English comic character, but her prologue and tale participate in a serious debate about the roles and proper behaviour of women that draws on such learned sources as St Jerome's Latin treatise *Adversus Jovinianum*.

Richard II (like Richard III) is one of those medieval kings who has suffered from the negative spin of the Tudor chroniclers. The popular image of him is derived from Shakespeare: a self-absorbed weakling who surrounded himself with flatterers, let the country go to rack and ruin, and had to be replaced in a *coup d'état* by strong-man Henry Bolingbroke, father of Henry V of glorious memory. In reality, Richard II presided over a court culture of great sophistication, in which Chaucer and his friend John Gower created a place for poetry.

Beyond the court, the nation was beginning to find its political voice, as witnessed by the Peasants' Revolt or 'Great Rising' of 1381 and the 'Lollard' project to modernize and democratize religion. The poem that was perceived to embody these developments was William Langland's *The Vision of Piers Plowman* (c. 1370–90). The fact that this long poem exists in several different versions and dozens of different manuscripts attests to its popularity and to the fact that Langland – about whom we know almost nothing – never stopped revising it (for instance by removing some of the more politically inflammatory passages after 1381).

The narrator of the poem falls asleep on the Malvern hills in the far west of England. He has a vision of a 'fair field full of folk': the people of England, for whom he writes of the quest for the saintly life, the corruption of the rich and powerful, and Jesus Christ's championing of the poor and the dispossessed. English rather than European, provincial as opposed to metropolitan in both dialect and outlook, pious rather than bawdy, Langland came to be perceived as Chaucer's great opposite. For John Ball in the Peasants' Revolt and again for the radical protestant 'commonwealth' men of the mid-16th century, the name of Piers Plowman became synonymous with sturdy English resistance to the tyranny, both monarchical and ecclesiastical, that came from the centres of power.

The Word of God

So when did English Literature begin? With the Celtic bards, with Julius Caesar, with Cædmon, with Alfred, with the poem that celebrated the battle of Brunanburh and Athelstan's unification of the kingdom? Or only with the evolution of the south-east dialect of Middle English embodied by Chaucer, which, though modified by the great vowel shift of the 16th century, became the basis of the received pronunciation of modern English – the so-called king's or queen's English? For the Elizabethans, it was Chaucer who was the father of English poetry, despite his own determined Europeanness.

Another way of answering the question is to say: in the beginning was the Word. English Literature came into being when the Word was made flesh in the English language. That is to say, when the most important book in the history of the world was translated into the vernacular.

Cædmon was the father of Old English biblical paraphrase. We may securely say that English Literature begins not with Homeric-style epic – praise of ancestors and demi-gods, heroes and warriors – but with Christian faith, with the praise of God. The Venerable Bede translated portions of the Bible. Aldhelm rendered the poetry of the Psalms into Old English in the late 7th century. In the 11th century, Ælfric took on great swathes of the Old Testament. In the 12th, a monk called Orm produced a mixture of selected translation and commentary. Then, crucially, came John Wyclif's 14th-century enterprise: the translation of the entire Bible from the Latin Vulgate into the vernacular. 'It helpeth Christian men', wrote Wyclif, to the consternation of the Church authorities, 'to study the Gospel in that tongue in which they know best Christ's sentence'.

The Bible tells of how the Word was made flesh when Jesus was born to the Virgin Mary. For women in the Middle Ages, the devotional example of Mary mother of God, of the women such as Mary Magdalene who loved Jesus, and of the female saints who were martyred in his name, were the inspiration to take up writing: literature by women in these islands has its origin in prayers and meditations, confessions of faith, songs of praise, and manuals of the contemplative life, such as the *Ancrene Wisse* (monastic rule for anchoresses, early 13th century), *Revelations of Divine Love* (mystical devotions of Julian of Norwich, late 14th century), and *The Book of Margery Kempe* (spiritual autobiography, early 15th century).

In the 16th century, English Protestants called themselves the 'people of the book'. The book they meant was the Bible. People of the book are perforce literary people. What is literature for? It is an attempt to give meaning to human life. That is also what the Bible is for. The ordering of our lives through *narrative*, through a structure of beginning, middle, and ending; the sense that individual details and events may be gathered into a pattern that forms a whole: in these conceptions, the Bible is literary and literature is biblical. 'The Old and New Testaments', wrote William Blake, 'are the Great Code of Art'.

Our primary tool for reading literature – hermeneutics, the art of interpretation – was originally devised as a way of reading the Bible. The Church Fathers taught the art of fourfold figural interpretation, in which the reader traces different strands of meaning: literal (historical), allegorical (higher, spiritual significance), tropological (the moral lesson), anagogical (to think of future and last things). The flexibility of this interpretative art has made it possible to read religious texts in secular ways and vice-versa. It has allowed pagan stories to be read allegorically in Christian terms, as in the medieval tradition of 'moralizing' the erotic tales of Ovid's *Metamorphoses*, thus resolving the dialectic of Hebrao-Christian and Greco-Roman traditions that has been one of the creative tensions energizing English Literature.

The Bible is also foundational of English Literature by virtue of its generic impurity. Its mix of mythology, history, and allegory, its parables, epistles, prophecies, poetry of praise (and even, in the *Song of Solomon*, of erotic love), are precedents for the stylistic variety of *The Canterbury Tales*, Shakespeare's collected plays, Wordsworth and Coleridge's *Lyrical Ballads*, James Joyce's *Ulysses*, and a thousand other hybrid creations.

Translation has always been central to English Literature not only because of the multiple languages of these islands, but also because it is central to the Bible itself. Jesus Christ and his disciples spoke Aramaic, but their Book was written in vernacular Greek, which was translated into Latin by Jerome (the so-called Vulgate), and has since been translated, and again and again re-translated, into English. The 1611 Authorized Version of the Bible, the exception which proves the rule of the old adage that no great literary work was ever written by a committee, was partly a response to what were perceived as the dangerous innovations of the Geneva translation undertaken by radical protestants a generation before, and of William Tyndale's translation prior to that. One of the demands among the instructions to the King James translators was 'The old ecclesiastical words to be kept, viz. as the word church not to be translated congregation'. The point here was that in Tyndale's version, *ecclesia* had been translated not as 'church' but as 'congregation'. Is the Church embodied in the ecclesiastical hierarchy or in the community of faith as a whole? This is at once a theological and a political question, and a matter of linguistic and literary interpretation.

As the Hebrew-Greek Bible itself consisted of stories from the past intended to be interpreted in the present and applied to human actions in the future, so every translation from Cædmon to the Authorized Version to the most recent updating has interpreted the ancient texts, been influenced by the historical forces of its own moment, and wagered upon its own future. The same may be said of the literary classics: writers respond to – in a broad sense, they 'translate' – a received body of works from the past in the light of their own present with the hope of being read in the future. In the case of the 1611 Bible, the wager paid off: no book had more influence on the English language and the English mind during the subsequent three and a half centuries.

Chapter 4
The study of English

Literature in education: from rhetoric to elocution

When Shakespeare went to school in the 16th century, John Milton in the 17th, and Samuel Johnson in the 18th, they would have studied literature, but not English Literature. The tools of linguistic and literary study – grammar, rhetoric (the organization of language for the purposes of forceful argument), and prosody (the metrical arrangements that constitute verse) – were at the centre of the curriculum. But what Shakespeare, Milton, and Johnson studied was the grammar of the Latin language, the oratory of Cicero, and the metrics of poets such as Virgil and Horace.

With the religious Reformation of the 16th century, there was a huge expansion of grammar school education for boys from the middle ranks of society. Grammar meant Latin grammar. The purpose of studying it was to give pupils the mastery of language. Rhetoric meant learning how to order your speeches: arguments in favour, arguments against, exemplification, testimony, conclusion. It meant honing your metaphors and developing elaborate figures of speech, learning by example hundreds of schemes (verbal patterns) and tropes (ingenious twists of meaning).

When Shakespeare's King Henry IV says 'Uneasy lies the head that wears a crown' he is using *metonymy*, a trope of substitution whereby 'head' stands for king and 'crown' for the idea of sovereignty. The resulting particularity is vivid and memorable, as a general statement would not be ('powerful people often find it hard to get to sleep'). When Milton begins his elegy 'Lycidas' with the line 'Yet once more, O ye Laurels, and once more', he is using *antimetabole*, a scheme in which the same words are repeated at the beginning and the end of a phrase. The echo effect makes the line easy to memorize. When Alexander Pope wishes to juxtapose the serious and the frivolous in *The Rape of the Lock*, he is assisted by a neat little figure called *zeugma*, whereby one verb looks after two nouns: 'Or stain her honour or her new brocade . . . Or lose her heart or necklace at a ball'. The rhetorical device creates the satirical effect. When Wordsworth looks down on the Vale of Chamonix in book six of *The Prelude* to behold 'A motionless array of mighty waves', he conjoins contradictory terms – how can a wave be motionless? The figure is *oxymoron*, ideal for evoking the paradoxes of perception.

Rhetoric shaped both thinking and compositional art. It was taught as preparation for a life of service to the state. Middle-class boys such as young Will Shakespeare and John Milton were given their training in the arts of language so that they could become lawyers and clerks and Church of England ministers and secretaries to politicians. But the Tudor educational revolution had an unintended consequence. Many of the brightest boys put their talents to very different uses: as poets, actors, and playwrights. Their plays and poems assisted in the work of nation-building by bringing alive the history and the myths that shaped the English people's sense of who they were, but by dramatizing the conflicts of both public and private life – tyrannical rulers being overthrown, arbiters of morality exposed as hypocrites, wives rebelling against their husbands – the poets and playwrights also made a huge contribution to the emergence of modern liberties.

English Literature itself did not become the object of formal academic study until the second half of the 18th century. When the philosopher Adam Smith was invited to deliver a series of public lectures on 'rhetoric and belles-lettres' in Edinburgh in the late 1740s, he broke with tradition by speaking in the English language and using vernacular as well as ancient Roman examples of rhetorical technique and fine writing. Hugh Blair followed Smith's example when in 1760 he was appointed to the position of Professor of Rhetoric and Belles-Lettres in the University of Edinburgh. Upon his retirement, Blair published his lectures and they went through dozens of editions, remaining the standard academic introduction to the art of literary criticism for more than half a century. They were especially widely studied in the United States.

In England, meanwhile, only men who subscribed to the articles of faith of the Church of England could attend the ancient universities of Oxford and Cambridge, where the language of instruction was Latin and the humanities side of the curriculum was confined to the ancients. Religious non-conformists or 'dissenters' accordingly set up academies of their own, where 'polite literature' ('belles-lettres') was taught in the English language. The teaching of what we now call English Literature was one of John Aikin's duties when he took up the tutorship in Belles-Lettres at the Warrington Academy in 1758. His daughter Anna Letitia Aikin (later Barbauld) grew up to become a popular and influential poet and editor, an apologist for the French Revolution, a passionate advocate of the abolition of the slave trade, and an important early analyst of the novel – her fifty-volume anthology *The British Novelists*, published in 1810, did more than any other publication to establish the repertoire of English fiction.

Aikin was succeeded in the literature tutorship at Warrington by the radical theologian and scientist Joseph Priestley, who also welcomed the French Revolution. From its very institutional origin, then, the discipline of English Literature was associated with dissent, with the democratization of education, and with resistance to the elitism of the established universities. It was helpful in this regard that the most sublime English poet was considered to be John Milton, author not only of the defining religious epic *Paradise Lost* but also of prose treatises in defence of the freedom of the press (*Areopagitica*, 1644) and the sovereign right of the people to depose their rulers (*The Tenure of Kings and Magistrates*, 1649).

The new discipline also provided educational opportunities for women. When Priestley left Warrington, the tutorship in Belles-Lettres passed to the Unitarian minister William Enfield, who created an anthology called *The Speaker* (1774), subtitled 'miscellaneous pieces, selected from the best English writers, and disposed under proper heads, with a view to facilitate the improvement of youth in reading and speaking'. This became the standard textbook for the teaching of eloquence and elocution in English throughout the land – at girls' schools as well as boys'. In 1811, Anna Barbauld published *The Female Speaker*, a companion volume specifically aimed at young women.

Enfield's categories of literature included narrative, didactic pieces (for instance, a series of passages from Alexander Pope's *Essay on Man* in rhyming couplets), orations and harangues (political speeches, some from modern parliament, others from Shakespeare), dialogues (mostly from drama, especially Shakespeare), descriptions (notably from 18th-century landscape poetry), and 'pathetic' pieces (examples of strong feeling, with a huge majority taken from Shakespeare, though some more modern, such as Yorick's death in *Tristram Shandy*). The idea was that a thorough grounding in these four hundred pages of extracts would improve the vocabulary and articulacy of pupils, while also cultivating their emotions and their moral sense.

Enfield laid the foundations for what Vicesimus Knox, compiler of a similar anthology (*Elegant Extracts*, 1783), called a 'liberal education'. Its beneficiaries were not the ruling class, who continued to be schooled in the Greek and Roman classics until well into the 20th century, but middle-class non-conformists, women, and soon the working classes (through radical Chartist educational projects and more conservative working men's colleges) and colonial subjects (beginning with the reform of Indian education in the 1830s). Looked at from one point of view, the teaching of elocution and the emergent discipline of English were intended to instil conformity of linguistic usage and moral values. But for non-conformist pupils in the dissenting academies, for Victorian labouring-class auto-didacts, for the first women to gain access to universities, for colonial subjects such as Gandhi and Nehru, and for mid-20th-century northern working-class grammar school boys and girls, the study of English Literature was as often a crucible of liberal thought and an engine of social mobility.

Criticism in the public sphere: Dr Johnson

The detailed analysis of English literary texts began not in the educational system, but in what has become known as 'the public sphere' – the realm of civil or 'polite' urban society that emerged in the 18th century, thriving in the new environments of newspaper and coffee-house.

The terms of debate had been established by John Dryden, sometimes called the father of English criticism, in the prefaces to, and essays about, his plays and poems, in which he had self-consciously set about modernizing and classicizing English writing during the Restoration era of the late 17th century. What were the relative merits of the ancients and the moderns, of native and continental models, of blank verse and rhyme? What was the correct balance between 'art' and 'nature', the best means to achieve verisimilitude? What ultimately constitutes good writing? As Dryden put it in his preface to *The State of Innocence* (1677), his dramatization of Milton's *Paradise Lost*, 'By criticism, as it was first instituted by Aristotle, was meant a standard of judging well; the chiefest part of which is, to observe those excellencies which should delight a reasonable reader'.

In *The Spectator* essays mainly by Joseph Addison (1711–14) and *The Tatler* mainly by Richard Steele (1709), questions of literary style were closely linked to debates about national identity and gentlemanly behaviour. Through the deliberations of the Shakespeare Ladies Club (1730s) and the publications of the Bluestockings (1750s onwards, led by Elizabeth Montagu), well-to-do women joined the conversation. But the figure who dominated literary debate in the public sphere in the second half of the 18th century was Dr Samuel Johnson.

Johnson judged books according to a few simple but firm principles. 'Nothing can please many, and please long, but just representations of general nature' (Preface to Shakespeare). 'The only end of writing is to enable the readers better to enjoy life, or better to endure it' (review of Soame Jenyns, *A Free Enquiry into the Nature and Origin of Evil*). 'In this work are exhibited in a very high degree the two most engaging powers of an author. New things are made familiar, and familiar things are made new' ('Life of Alexander Pope'). His opinions carried weight by virtue of the sheer force of his language.

The son of a bookseller, he dropped out of Oxford because he was unable to pay the fees. He began his career as a schoolmaster. The school failed and he walked from Lichfield to London with his pupil David Garrick, who would become the greatest actor of the age, perhaps of any age. Johnson's admiration for him knew no bounds, yet he always harboured doubts about the theatre. This was partly because it was hard for the sometime master to find himself struggling to forge a living from his pen in Grub Street while the pupil found wealth and unprecedented fame on the boards. But it was also because the actor's art of flighty impersonation was at odds with the supreme Johnsonian virtues of integrity and sincerity.

In the preface to his earliest work, a translation of a traveller's tale, Johnson noted how the story revealed that human nature is the same in every nation. In every individual and every community we find 'a mixture of vice and virtue, a contest of passion and reason'. Johnson was steadfast in his pursuit of virtue and reason, whilst never denying his own vices and the power of his passions. He knew humankind's need for a moral and spiritual compass, but also recognized the force of our bodily desires.

The Spectator and *The Tatler* of Addison and Steele had fallen by the wayside, so Johnson single-handedly revived the essay as a literary genre with *The Rambler*, in which he pronounced twice weekly (publication Tuesdays and Saturdays) on books, on politics, on morals, on life. A High Church Anglican, who wrestled with his conscience and his melancholy in prayers and meditations of deep humility, Johnson found both personal comfort and political wisdom in the words of Jesus. In building a theory of rights on the basis of the Sermon on the Mount, he became zealous against every form of slavery. Invited back to Oxford as a celebrity, he shocked the dons with his post-prandial toast 'Here's to the next insurrection of the negroes in the West Indies'. He carried his principles into his private life, taking a motley assortment of waifs and strays into his household. And loving them. In his will, he left the bulk of his estate to 'Francis Barber, my man-servant, a negro'.

He was a man of prodigious industry, who single-handedly compiled *A Dictionary of the English Language*:

ADAMS [Oxford don] But, Sir, how can you do this in three years?

JOHNSON Sir, I have no doubt that I can do it in three years.

ADAMS But the French Academy, which consists of forty members, took forty years to compile their Dictionary.

JOHNSON Sir, thus it is. This is the proportion. Let me see; forty times forty is sixteen hundred. As three to sixteen hundred, so is the proportion of an Englishman to a Frenchman.

To be fair, the *Dictionary* took him eight years. But that was no reason for him to berate himself for sloth, as he constantly did.

No sooner had he finished the *Dictionary* than he set to work on a new edition of the complete plays of Shakespeare, with commentary. Literary criticism in Johnson's time was dominated by French precepts. Johnson's riposte was English common sense. Where the French tangled themselves in the rules of art, Johnson's only principle was truth to life. Voltaire threw up his hands in *horreur* at Shakespeare's mingling of tragedy and comedy, kings and clowns. Johnson replies that that is how life is:

> Shakespeare's plays are not in the rigorous and critical sense either tragedies or comedies, but compositions of a distinct kind; exhibiting the real state of sublunary nature, which partakes of good and evil, joy and sorrow, mingled with endless variety of proportion and innumerable modes of combination ... in which, at the same time, the reveler is hasting to his wine, and the mourner burying his friend.

Johnson lived through an age of financial speculation, unprecedented consumer spending, and a rampant press. The new power of the press gave birth to a celebrity culture: the antics of actresses and courtesans filled the gossip columns, while Garrick was the first genuinely international star actor. It was also an age of fierce political debate. Thanks to satirical writers and artists, some Irish (Jonathan Swift) and others homegrown (Alexander Pope, John Gay, William Hogarth, Johnson himself), literature played a vital part in exposing, excoriating, and ridiculing the hypocrisy of those who jostled for power and influence. Johnson's breakthrough in Grub Street came from his work as a parliamentary sketch writer. Since there were reporting restrictions on what was actually said in parliament, he took to making up the speeches and putting them into the mouths of the honourable members. His column in *The Gentleman's Magazine* was called, with a nod to Swift, *Reports of the Debates in the Senate of Lilliput.*

In and around the life and work of Dr Johnson, we find many of the things that continued to be definitive of 'Englishness' for a further two centuries: the richness of the language, admiration for Shakespeare, a refusal to be bullied and bossed around, a sense of humour and of the ridiculous, good classical actors, a love of gossip and an interest in the quirkiness of individual lives (Johnson's *Lives of the Poets* offered a pioneering mix of criticism and biography), robust opinions and melancholy realism, the capacity to survive so long as there is access to a cup of tea.

The public sphere of the 19th and 20th centuries allowed ample space for debates about literature. There is a line of descent from Francis Jeffrey in the *Edinburgh Review* (founded 1802), through Matthew Arnold and Walter Pater in the Victorian era, to T. S. Eliot's *Criterion* in the 1920s, to Virginia Woolf writing in the *Times Literary Supplement*, to George Orwell broadcasting on the BBC during the Second World War, to A. Alvarez publishing and reviewing poetry in *The Observer* (1956–66). Most of the literary opinion-formers were creative writers themselves, and in this sense they were authorities in the tradition of Dryden and Johnson. With the 21st-century migration of the media to cyberspace, the free-for-all that characterizes the blogosphere and the online reader review in which everyone is a critic, there has been a sharp decline of deference to authoritative opinion. In one sense, this is a further democratization of the process that began in the chatrooms of the 18th-century coffee-house; in another, it represents the collapse of the idea of a Johnsonian public sphere underwritten by common sense and core moral values.

Aesthetics versus history

In 1774, a London non-conformist man of letters called William Kenrick published a proposal to establish 'A Public Academy, for the Investigation of the English Language, and the Illustration of British Literature', but the scheme did not come to fruition. Lectures on English Literature of the kind that are now delivered in universities only came into being in the early 19th century. The pioneers of this genre were the poet-philosopher Samuel Taylor Coleridge (son of a Church of England country clergyman and educated at Cambridge University) and the radical journalist William Hazlitt (son of a leading non-conformist minister and educated at the Hackney dissenting academy). During the Regency period (1811–20), Coleridge and Hazlitt delivered several rival series of lectures, Coleridge at the genteel venue of the Royal Institution just off Piccadilly in central London, Hazlitt at the non-conformist Surrey Institution in a more down-at-heel location on the south bank of the River Thames.

Coleridge was deeply interested in the *theory* of literature, as developed in the new philosophy of beauty called 'aesthetics' that had emerged in late 18th-century Germany. He adapted many of his theories from German thinkers. A. W. von Schlegel, for example, gave him the idea that whereas works of literature based on neoclassical rules were merely 'mechanical', truly original writing was 'organic', shaped by a form that grew from within.

In parallel with his lectures, Coleridge developed his theory of literature in *Biographia Literaria*. 'The imagination, or esemplastic power', he says there, is 'the living power and prime agent of all human perception'. 'Esemplastic' means the power of shaping disparate things into one. The Coleridgean imagination is nothing less than 'a repetition in the finite mind of the eternal act of creation in the infinite I AM'. Here poetry is defined as imagination wrought to its uttermost:

> The poet, described in ideal perfection, brings the whole soul of man into activity . . . He diffuses a tone and spirit of unity, that blends, and (as it were) fuses, each into each, by that synthetic and magical power, to which I would exclusively appropriate the name of Imagination. This power . . . reveals itself in the balance or reconciliation of opposite or discordant qualities: of sameness, with difference; of the general with the concrete; the idea with the image;

the individual with the representative; the sense of novelty and freshness with old and familiar objects; a more than usual state of emotion with more than usual order; judgment ever awake and steady self-possession with enthusiasm and feeling profound or vehement; and while it blends and harmonizes the natural and the artificial, still subordinates art to nature; the manner to the matter; and our admiration of the poet to our sympathy with the poetry.

(Biographia Literaria, 1817)

Coleridge coined the term 'practical criticism' for the art of testing individual poems against these demanding principles. A century later, the academic I. A. Richards made this art into the central feature of the influential Cambridge University school of English studies. Poems and passages of prose were read with close attention and analysed according to their success or failure in balancing or reconciling opposite or discordant qualities, in holding together more than usual emotion and more than usual order. The very greatest works were judged to be those that succeeded in saying contradictory things at the same time and finding some sort of complex resolution. Richards' most dazzling pupil, William Empson, could find *Seven Types of Ambiguity* (1930) within a single text by Shakespeare or John Donne.

Hazlitt's *Lectures on the English Poets* (1818) also characterized literary excellence in aesthetic terms, giving John Keats, who was in the audience, the germ of his idea of 'negative capability' ('that is when man is capable of being in uncertainties, Mysteries, doubts, without any irritable reaching after fact and reason'). But in the first of his *Lectures chiefly on the Dramatic Literature of the Age of Elizabeth*, delivered the following year and published in 1820, Hazlitt took a different approach, relating literature to its historical context.

He argued that the first cause of the remarkable flowering of literary creativity in England in the late 16th century was the religious Reformation, which 'gave a mighty impulse and increased activity to thought and inquiry, and agitated the inert mass of accumulated prejudices throughout Europe'. The translation of the Bible into the vernacular 'was the chief engine in the great work'. Combined with the Reformation, there was a renaissance of the classics: 'round about the same time, the rich and fascinating stores of the Greek and Roman mythology, and those of the romantic poetry of Spain and Italy, were eagerly explored by the curious, and thrown open in translations to the admiring gaze of the vulgar'. 'What also gave an unusual *impetus* to the mind of man at this period', continues Hazlitt, 'was the discovery of the New World, and the reading of voyages and travels.' And then there was the birth of the public playhouse: 'The stage was a new thing; and those who had to supply its demands laid their hands upon whatever came within their reach.' Hazlitt relished the rich and energizing eclecticism of the drama of the period, its joyous mingling of high matter and low, verse and prose, kings and clowns.

The birthpangs of Protestantism, the renewed reception of the ancients, the expansion of geographical horizons, and the new profession of theatre were all essential to the flowering of English literature in the late 16th century. But Hazlitt added a fifth factor, under which he attempted to subsume the first four: he claimed that 'the natural genius of the country' never 'shone out fuller or brighter, or looked more like itself, than at this period'.

The proposition that England was somehow more itself in the time of Elizabeth I than before or since, a claim closely linked to the cult of the queen herself as greatest of all English monarchs, has often been used to goad or to exhort the Britain of the present. In the 1730s, opponents of Sir Robert Walpole, the first modern prime minister, developed a politics of nostalgia that looked to the Elizabethan example for support of a more aggressive foreign policy and a defence of the English landed interest over the British trading one. From a very different political perspective, Hazlitt's own nostalgia for the freedom from tyranny which he saw

English Literature

embodied in the Reformation was the consequence of his deep disillusionment with the defeat of the French Revolution and the ultra-reactionary policies of the British government in the post-Waterloo years during which he delivered his lectures.

More than most who have used the language of patriotism, Hazlitt was diffident about doing so, hedging his account of the national character around with a 'perhaps' and an 'if I may so speak without offence or flattery'. He was aware that to bring forward the idea of the natural genius of his island race was to offer a different order of explanation from the factual. The break with Rome happened; the classics were translated and the Italian influence received; Drake and Ralegh sailed the oceans; the Burbages built their playhouse. But a national character is something that has to be invented. For that matter, so does a nation. It might be truer to say that Elizabethan literature created a character for the nation than that a national character created Elizabethan literature.

Ever since Plato and Aristotle began theorizing about poetry and drama in ancient Greece, literature has occupied a place somewhere between philosophy and history. Philosophically minded critics such as Coleridge have been interested in the structural properties and symbolic logic of literary works; politically minded critics such as Hazlitt have been more interested in the ways in which literary works embody or resist what he called 'the spirit of the age'. Coleridge and Hazlitt drew the battle-lines between 'formalist' and 'historicist' criticism, an opposition that has recurred in literature's many 'theory wars' in the two centuries since they delivered their lectures.

Literary criticism is at its most interesting when it holds together three different impulses identified by Matthew Arnold in his critical essays a generation after Coleridge and Hazlitt. Disinterested formalism: 'to see the object as in itself it really is'. Historical judgement: 'to try books as to the influence they are calculated to have upon the general culture of single nations or the world at large'. And, more polemically, considered evangelism on behalf of 'culture' (which to Arnold meant playfulness and liberality of mind as well as 'high seriousness') against 'philistinism' (complacent moralizing, smug provinciality): 'to learn and propagate the best that is known and thought in the world'.

From writer to reader

'I wish our clever young poets would remember my homely definitions of prose and poetry', begins an entry in Coleridge's *Table Talk*, dated 12 July 1827, 'prose – words in their best order; poetry – the best words in their best order'. If writers take the trouble to choose the best words and put them in their best order, readers owe literary texts the respect of attentiveness to particular verbal choices, and students of English need to have confidence that they are reading the right words. But the road from the moment of literary composition with quill or pen, typewriter or word-processing package, to the act of reading is a complicated one in which authorial second thoughts, editorial interventions, and printing-house mishaps all play a part.

The work of establishing accurate texts has accordingly been an important part of the history of English studies. In the 18th century, scholars began emending and annotating the works of Shakespeare and Milton, using procedures that had been developed for the editing of the Greek and Latin classics. Lewis Theobald's rigorous treatment of Shakespeare's texts led Alexander Pope, a less scholarly editor of Shakespeare, to make him king of the Dunces in a mock epic that was published as a parody of an over-annotated scholarly edition (*The Dunciad*, 1728–9). But this did not stop the Cambridge University classical scholar Richard Bentley from publishing soon after an edition of *Paradise Lost* replete with emendations supported by learned explanations. So, for example, Bentley could not believe that the great Milton intended something so indecorously oxymoronic as 'darkness visible'. He emended the phrase to 'transpicuous gloom'.

The most renowned character in the history of English Literature is Shakespeare's Hamlet. In his restlessness and his thoughtfulness, his wrestling with his conscience and his memory, the tensions between his private and public selves, the conflict between his roles as son and lover, he seems to embody modern Western man's questioning of what it means to be human. Into his solo speeches (soliloquies), we project the sanctity of our own inner lives, our freedom to think what we will, our right even to choose death. Hamlet, as he acknowledges himself, is made of 'words, words, words'. But how confident can we be that we know the words out of which Shakespeare wrote him?

Consider the most famous line in English Literature. *Hamlet* was first published in 1603, in a pocket format volume known as a quarto (eight pages of text were printed on large sheets of paper, which were then folded two times to produce four leaves, so each leaf was a quarter the size of the original sheet). The title page read *The tragicall historie of Hamlet Prince of Denmarke by William Shake-speare. As it hath been diuerse times acted by his Highnesse seruants in the cittie of London: as also in the two vniuersities of Cambridge and Oxford, and else-where* (in the early modern printing-house 'v'/'u' and 'i'/'j' were interchangeable). In this First Quarto, Hamlet's meditation on life and death begins 'To be, or not to be, I there's the point'. 'I' is a variant spelling of 'Ay', meaning 'yes'.

A year later, a Second Quarto was published with the title page, *The tragicall historie of Hamlet, Prince of Denmarke. By William Shakespeare. Newly imprinted and enlarged to almost as much againe as it was, according to the true and perfect coppie.* This was as if to say: if you purchased the First Quarto last year, you are in possession of a highly defective copy, including not much more than half the script, and full of false or imperfect readings, whereas what you are now being offered is the full, authorized text. Hamlet's soliloquy now begins in the form that has become familiar: 'To be, or not to be, that is the question'.

The large-format and expensive 1623 First Folio of Shakespeare's collected plays prints a text of *Hamlet* that has many variants from the quartos. Here, the opening of 'To be, or not to be' is the same as in the Second Quarto, save that 'Question' has an initial capital and the line ends with a colon, denoting a heavy pause, instead of a comma, denoting a light one. Later in the speech, there are numerous variants, most notably the repeated substitution of 'heaven' for 'God'. Second Quarto and Folio also agree that Hamlet speaks these lines after the arrival of the players at Elsinore in what the Folio calls the third act of the play (there are no act divisions in the quartos). In the First Quarto, however, Hamlet's soliloquy had occurred at an earlier point in the action, when he enters reading upon a book.

English Literature

In the absence of Shakespeare's original manuscripts, the journey from his writing of the lines through the first performances of the play to the early printed editions can only be traced via conjectural reconstruction, based on surviving evidence about the writing habits of Elizabethan playwrights, the fluidity of scripts within the theatrical repertoire, and the practices of the early modern printing-house. Though there is still fierce academic debate over the status of the three early texts of *Hamlet*, most scholars now agree that the First Quarto gives us a glimpse of an early performance text of the play, the Second Quarto takes us close to Shakespeare's full script, and the First Folio represents the authoritative performance text of his acting company, the Chamberlain's (later King's) Men, incorporating theatrical revisions and an element of censorship as a result of a parliamentary act that prohibited the speaking of the word 'God' on stage.

The publication of the early texts was the beginning of another journey, in which the play was passed to readers and theatre companies in later ages. Textual transmission is the first prerequisite for the endurance of literary works through history. Without editions, there would be no Shakespeare. Without editors, there would be no texts for study in the classroom.

A key editorial decision, which becomes especially contentious in the case of multiple-origin works such as *Hamlet*, is the choice of a base text from which to begin the process. Some variants between the early texts of Shakespeare's plays can be explained by the faulty memory of an actor or the erroneous typesetting of a printer, but others are the result of authorial or playhouse revision. In such cases, it is hard to choose between the original version and the revised versions. The differences between the early texts of *King Lear* are so substantive that some editors consider it worthwhile to print Quarto and Folio in parallel, just as the variant 1805 and 1850 texts of Wordsworth's *The Prelude* are sometimes printed in modern scholarly editions.

There is no definitive text of Shakespeare. A thoroughgoing process of editorial mediation has been interposed between writer and reader. Though the particular conditions of Shakespeare's career as a working playwright make him a notoriously hard case, there is hardly any major literary author who does not throw up editorial problems of one sort or another.

The Canterbury Tales survives in more than eighty scribal manuscripts, all dating from after Chaucer's death. Nobody knows whether Chaucer ever completed his project. The original plan, mentioned in the General Prologue, for each pilgrim to tell two tales on the way to Canterbury and two on the way back, was certainly not fulfilled. Many variants between the early manuscripts can be accounted for by scribal error, but others may be the result of authorial revision. Different manuscripts have very different orderings of the narrative sequence. Some tales clearly belong together: the bawdy fable of the Miller's Tale as a contrast to the high courtly romance of the Knight's, the cuckolding of a miller in the Reeve's Tale as revenge for that of a carpenter (the reeve's former trade) in the Miller's. Others are inter-related via allusions in the linking passages between tales. But the positioning of many of the tales must be decided by editorial judgement, a process that has been ongoing since William Caxton produced the first printed text of the *Canterbury Tales* in the 1470s (based on a text that does not correspond to any surviving manuscript).

In order to be readable, a printed edition has to choose a single text or at most two or three variant texts printed in parallel or in sequence. In theory, a hypertext electronic edition can bring together every surviving text of a classic work. Eighty different versions of *The Canterbury Tales* could be compared with the click of a mouse. The advent of digitized texts does not, however, put an end to editorial mediation. A decision still has to be made as to which text to prioritize on the home page as a starting point. Furthermore, mass digitization projects such as Google Books have proceeded indiscriminately, with alarmingly little rigour in determination of the relative authority of particular texts. One of the first such projects, the publisher Chadwyck-Healey's LION (Literature Online) database, has created an invaluable library of English poetry and drama, but an editorial decision to omit prose 'paratexts' – dedications, prefaces, commentary notes, and the like – from the digitized texts seriously distorts their original form.

Facsimile reproduction is the best way of representing the original form of early texts. It is especially helpful for rendering visual effects. Thus a facsimile of George Herbert's poem 'Easter Wings' (1633) makes much more sense than the poem as it is printed in many editions and anthologies, where it is rotated through ninety degrees, losing the effect of a bird's, and hence an angel's, wings.

A photographic facsimile or a text that rigorously follows, say, the first edition, will still leave many editorial problems unsolved. Take the case of Dickens' *Great Expectations* (1861). The novelist Wilkie Collins, a close friend of Dickens, objected to the original ending in which Estella remarries and Pip remains single. Dickens accordingly revised to a more conventional ending, which suggests that Pip and Estella will marry. 'I have put in as pretty a little piece of writing as I could', he explained, 'and I have no doubt the story will be more acceptable through the

¶ Easter wings.

¶ Easter wings.

Lord, who createdst man in wealth and store,
Though foolishly he lost the same,
Decaying more and more,
Till he became
Most poore:
With thee
O let me rise
As larks, harmoniously,
And sing this day thy victories:
Then shall the fall further the flight in me.

My tender age in sorrow did beginne
And still with sicknesse and shame
Thou didst so punish sinne,
That I became
Most thinne.
With thee
Let me combine,
And feel this day thy victorie:
For, if I imp my wing on thine,
Affliction shall advance the flight in me.

3. 'Easter Wings' in George Herbert, *The Temple* (1633). Rotated through ninety degrees in many modern editions, such as the *Norton Anthology of English Literature*, thus losing the wing effect

alteration'. But he did not feel entirely sure that he had done the right thing: 'Upon the whole I think it is for the better.' Most editions publish the second ending, but Dickens' friend and biographer John Forster preferred the first, as have many of the novel's most distinguished readers (George Gissing, George Bernard Shaw, George Orwell, Edmund Wilson, Angus Wilson). On the other hand, the revised version has the merit of a certain ambiguity in keeping with the uncertainties that run throughout the novel's plot. The closing line, 'I saw no shadow of another parting from her' may mean that Pip and Estella will marry, but it might also mean that they will never see each other again. In this instance, we really need to consider both endings and to debate their relative merits.

Thomas Hardy published an explanatory note with the first American edition of *Tess of the d'Urbervilles* (1892): 'The main portion of the following story appeared – with slight modifications – in the *Graphic* newspaper and *Harper's Bazaar*; other chapters, more especially addressed to adult readers, in the *Fortnightly*

Review and the *National Observer*, as episodic sketches.' As if this were not complicated enough, the American serial publication texts differ in many particulars from the British, and the American first edition differs in other respects from the British. The respective proof texts are different from each other and from the published texts. Numerous later editions incorporated revisions by Hardy. The variants between the many different versions of *Tess* run the gamut from censorship imposed by magazine editors to conscious authorial revision for aesthetic effect. There is no single, authoritative text of this or any other Thomas Hardy novel.

Nor should we imagine that questions of textual variation have disappeared in the modern age, in which the printing of books from digital files prepared by authors themselves has removed several of the intervening agents, such as the printing-house typesetter, who in past years have been responsible for intentionally or unintentionally altering texts as they pass from writer to reader. Consider the following in the first British edition of Ian McEwan's novella *On Chesil Beach* (2007): 'He played her "clumsy but honourable" cover versions of Chuck Berry songs by the Beatles and the Rolling Stones.' This sentence does not appear in the first American edition or the British paperback edition, which appeared the following year. The reason? Not a printer's error, but an eagle-eyed reviewer's observation that at the time when the scene is set in the early 1960s, neither the Beatles nor the Rolling Stones had yet recorded any cover versions of Chuck Berry songs. Believing that this factual error diminished the verisimilitude of his fictional tale, McEwan ordered its removal. This will present a tricky choice should there ever come a time when a scholar is charged with the preparation of an authoritative edition of the collected novels of Ian McEwan.

Editorial choices are interpretive choices. They not only provide the necessary foundation for the survival of the classics: they also exemplify the act of thoughtful, attentive reading that literature asks of us.

Chapter 5
Periods and movements

Literature and national character

Historians of the 19th century believed that the evolution of the
manners and mentalities of a nation could be traced through its
literature. Books from the past came to be perceived as traces of the
culture out of which they emerged, to be regarded in a manner
analogous to fossils in the new science of geology. The first
comprehensive attempt to track the development of English
civilization via its literature was undertaken by a Frenchman,
Hippolyte Taine, in a four-volume *Histoire de la littérature
anglaise*, published in 1864 and based on the categories of race,
historical moment, and environment (*milieu*). 'A literary work',
wrote Taine,

> is not a mere play of the imagination, the isolated caprice of an
> excited brain, but a transcript of contemporary manners and
> customs and the sign of a particular state of intellect. The conclusion
> derived from this is that, through literary monuments, we can
> retrace the way in which men and women felt and thought many
> centuries ago.

Taine's narrative structure shaped the study of English literary
history for a hundred years. He began with the Saxons, the
Normans, and then the Chaucerian moment in which the

English language became the dominant literary medium for the first time. His second section was called 'The Renaissance', giving weight to the influences that Hazlitt discerned in the Elizabethan age.

Then came the 'The Classic Age', beginning with the Restoration of 1660. Here Taine argued that there was a symbiosis between the decisive shift of power from monarchy to parliament inaugurated by the Glorious Revolution of 1688 and the emergence in manners and in literature of 'the empire of a serious, reflective, moral spirit, capable of discipline and independence, which can alone maintain and give effect to a constitution'. Though the word 'empire' is suggestive of a vision of monolithic nationalism, Taine was acutely alert to political difference. He developed a sustained contrast between the anguished Tory Jonathan Swift and the serene Whig Joseph Addison, suggesting that England became modern and achieved its political and moral standing by virtue of the way in which its literary culture sustained the spirit of debate between them. Democracy, by this account, is the art of civilized disagreement.

Taine's fourth section was called 'Modern Life'. It focused on 'The Romantic School', singling out Lord Byron as 'the greatest and most English of these artists . . . so great that from him alone we shall learn more truths of his country and of his age than from all the rest together'. Above all in his burlesque epic *Don Juan* (1819–24), which Taine describes as a 'conversation' and a 'confidence', Byron is 'inexhaustibly fertile and creative', giving voice to every conceivable emotion and idea, even as he is preyed upon by 'the malady of the age', the sense that happiness is impossible, truth unattainable, society inequitable, and 'man abortive or marred'. Taine then concluded with a survey of the 'Modern Authors' who were still alive as he wrote, judging presciently that the novel would come to be regarded as the genre formative of the Victorian age, with Charles Dickens its foremost exponent.

Periodization

Taine's narrative laid the ground for the periodization that has dominated English literary history ever since: the Anglo-Saxon era; the medieval period, from 1066 to the early 16th century; the Renaissance, sometimes now referred to as the 'early modern' period, from the Reformation to the Restoration; the 'classical' period, from the 1660s to the 1780s, often known as the Enlightenment (a reference to the philosophical tenor of the times) or the Augustan age (on account of the way that leading writers such as Alexander Pope self-consciously compared their culture to that of ancient Rome under the emperor Augustus); Romanticism, from the French Revolution to the 1830s; the Victorian age; then, after Taine, the Modernism of the early 20th century.

There have been many debates about exactly when each new literary movement began. Was Romanticism foreshadowed by the youthful genius of Thomas Chatterton, the 'sensibility' of William Cowper, or the *Elegiac Sonnets* (1784) of Charlotte Smith? Modernism anticipated by the 'sprung rhythm' of Gerard Manley Hopkins or the urban impressionism of Amy Levy and Arthur Symons? But there can be no doubt that at various moments in literary history there have been concerted attempts to 'make it new' (Ezra Pound's phrase). Elizabethan critics such as William Webbe and George Puttenham heralded the triumph of the English language over Latin. John Dryden and his contemporaries believed that they were modernizing that language, introducing new plainness, rigour, and clarity to English verse. Victorian intellectuals such as Thomas Carlyle, Matthew Arnold, and John Ruskin believed that literature was a uniquely powerful vehicle for reading the signs of their own times, for interpreting and learning to live with, on the one hand, the 'march of progress' – urbanization, industrialization, railways, commercial travellers, empire – and, on the other, the 'melancholy, long, withdrawing roar' of the 'Sea of Faith' (Arnold, 'Dover Beach') as it retreated over the sands of biblical criticism, evolutionary science, and modern scepticism.

In a poem called 'Three Movements', published in 1932, W. B. Yeats identified the expanding horizons of the Shakespearean moment, the self-expression of the Romantic revolution, and the trauma of his own time as the great turning points in cultural and literary history. Renaissance, Romanticism, Modernism: these are the three movements that have been most studied and most often regarded as the high watermarks of the tide of English Literature. At each historical moment, clusters of writers, who often knew each other, pushed the boundaries of almost every genre of English Literature: Sidney, Spenser, Marlowe, Shakespeare, Jonson, Donne, Herbert, Middleton, Marston, Webster, then Milton and Marvell, during the Renaissance of the late 16th and 17th centuries; Blake, William and Dorothy Wordsworth, Coleridge, Charlotte Smith, Scott, Byron, Percy and Mary Shelley, Keats, and Clare during the Romantic revolution of the late 18th and early 19th centuries; Eliot, Pound, Yeats, Joyce, Ford Madox Ford, Dorothy Richardson, Wyndham Lewis, Woolf, D. H. and T. E. Lawrence, Waugh, Aldous Huxley, and many more during the years from about 1910 to the outbreak of the Second World War. The labels Renaissance, Romantic, and Modernist were, however, attached after the event, not by the innovators themselves.

Renaissance

Humanist scholars of the 16th century argued that their age was witnessing new light and rebirth after a long period of cultural darkness. The vocabulary associated with this idea proposed a tripartite division between the enlightened 'ancients' of Greece and Rome, the benighted 'Middle Ages', and the 'moderns' in whom the values of the ancients were reborn. The idea goes back to Petrarch in 14th-century Italy, but it was only in the 19th century that our familiar nomenclature was found for the latter two divisions. After the decline of classical Rome came the *medieval* ('middle era') period. Thus John Ruskin in the fourth of his 1854 lectures on architecture: 'You have, then, the three periods: Classicalism, extending to the fall of the Roman empire; Mediaevalism, extending from that fall to the close of the fifteenth century; and Modernism.' Ruskin's assertion that, in northern Europe at least, the modern era began at the close of the 15th century was widespread, but the term favoured above modernism was *Renaissance*, a word which was first used in France by Jules Michelet, which reached England in the 1840s, which Matthew Arnold in *Culture and Anarchy* (1869) attempted to Anglicize as 'Renascence', and which achieved wide currency through Jacob Burckhardt's *The Civilization of the Renaissance in Italy* (1860) and Walter Pater's *The Renaissance* (1873). Pater made clear that the word referred not merely to the re-birth – from French *renaître* – of the ancients, but to 'a whole complex movement of which that revival of classical antiquity was but one element or symptom'. The 19th-century understanding of this movement may be summed up in a phrase that Burckhardt borrowed from Michelet: the discovery of the world and the discovery of man.

The English have traditionally been regarded as having far greater distinction in literature and theatre than in painting, sculpture, and music. Burckhardt's civilization of the Renaissance in Italy was embodied in the visual arts – Michelangelo, Raphael, Donatello, Piero della Francesca. The English Renaissance, by contrast, was associated with the poets and playwrights of the reign of Queen Elizabeth I (1558–1603). This meant that whereas the art of the Italian Renaissance was closely associated with Roman Catholicism, the literature of the English Renaissance emerged out of an aggressively Protestant environment. In the *Art of English Poesy* (1589), written in the immediate wake of the defeat of the Spanish Armada, George Puttenham located the origins of the Elizabethan literary efflorescence in the precise period when the religious Reformation began in England:

In the latter end of [Henry VIII]'s reign sprang up a new company of courtly makers, of whom Sir Thomas Wyatt the elder and Henry Earl of Surrey were the two chieftains, who having travelled into Italy, and there tasted the sweet and stately measures and style of the Italian Poesy, as novices crept out of the schools of Dante, Ariosto, and Petrarch, they greatly polished our rude and homely manner of vulgar Poesy from that it had been before, and for that cause may justly be said the first reformers of our English metre and style.

Here the word 'reformers' is removed from its ecclesiastical origins and given over to literary history. The emphasis on reform reveals the ideology behind the new literary aesthetic promoted by Puttenham: the break from Rome has created the imperative to forge a national cultural identity.

From Spenser to Milton to Marvell, much of the best poetry of the age was shaped by the creative clash of 'Renaissance' (classical, pagan) and 'Reformation' (biblical, protestant) values. John Milton honed his art in a masque for aristocratic performance at Ludlow Castle that became known as *Comus* (1637): it luxuriates in Shakespearean lyricism and classical mythology whilst simultaneously packing a moral punch, a combination that came to be the Miltonic hallmark. 'Lycidas' (1638), his elegy on a fellow Cambridge student whom he hardly knew, is at once a brilliant imitation of classical pastoral ('Weep no more, woeful shepherds, weep no more') and an assault on the corruption of the English clergy. *Paradise Lost*, the acme of English epic, is equally steeped in Virgil and Ovid on the one hand, the Bible and Milton's own treatise concerning Christian doctrine on the other.

Like Spenser before him, Milton was profoundly equivocal about creative art. As Spenser gave some of his most sensuous poetry to the temptress in the Bower of Bliss that Sir Guyon intemperately destroys, so Milton the poet put into the mouths of Satan and Eve seductive words that Milton the theologian knew were perilous. *Paradise Lost* shaped 18th-century poetry's taste for the sublime and its movement away from rhyme towards blank verse. But it also shaped the reaction against 18th-century decorum. The poets who came to be called the Romantics were obsessed not only with Milton's grand style but also with the charismatic figure of Satan, with the idea of Milton as 'a true Poet, and of the Devil's party without knowing it'. From Renaissance to Romanticism: a poet who thought that he was inspired by the spirit of God came to inspire poets who thought that they were inspired by the breeze of pure creativity.

Romanticism

Romanticism emerged in Germany in the late 18th century as a reaction against the dominance of French neoclassical culture. Across the continent, poets committed themselves to the overthrowing of the old cultural order even as they were ambivalent in their reaction to the political revolution that began in France in 1789. Jean-Jacques Rousseau laid some of the intellectual foundations for the French Revolution, but his more distinctive legacy was the cult of sensibility. After Rousseau, it became acceptable even for Englishmen to cry. Powdered wigs were thrown away and women's dresses flowed with the contours of their bodies. Goethe's passionate novel, *The Sorrows of Young Werther* (1774), which A. W. von Schlegel splendidly described as 'a declaration of the rights of feeling', allegedly inspired a wave of copycat suicides. Sentiment was the order of the day.

In 1798, under the imprint of a minor provincial publisher, a slender volume of poetry was published with no author's name on the cover and the unassuming title *Lyrical Ballads, with a few other poems*. Twenty years later, it was recognized as the point of ignition for English Literature's Romantic revolution. William Hazlitt looked back on 1798 as an epoch in his life. In a vivid essay called 'My first acquaintance with poets', he remembered the privilege of meeting the two authors of the collection, the as yet little-known William Wordsworth and Samuel Taylor Coleridge.

They read aloud some of the poems. Hazlitt recalled that 'The sense of a new style and a new spirit in poetry came over me. It had to me something of the effect that arises from the turning up of the fresh soil, or of the first welcome breath of Spring.'

The literary establishment did not share Hazlitt's enthusiasm. The reception of *Lyrical Ballads* was initially lukewarm. Wordsworth was frustrated. His purposes had not been understood. So it was that in 1800, when the collection was reissued together with a second volume of new poems, he wrote a long preface. It was his manifesto for the new poetry of feeling. His aim in the poems, he said, had been to explore 'the manner in which we associate ideas in a state of excitement', to examine how human beings behave at times of extreme emotional stress. In particular, he had sought to tap into some of the fundamental passions that the urbane and polished poetry of the previous century had all too often neglected. The 'maternal passion', for instance, the subject of 'The Idiot Boy' and 'The Mad Mother', or 'the perplexity and obscurity which in childhood attend our notion of death, or rather our utter inability to admit that notion', an idea wonderfully conveyed by the ballad 'We Are Seven', in which an adult confronts a little girl, one of a family of seven children, two of whom have died. To the calculating adult, 'If two are in the churchyard laid, / Then ye are only five', but to the child who sits and sings to her siblings in the grave, there is no acknowledgement of death: 'Nay, we are seven!' Motherhood, children, death. Wordsworth saw that to bring the three together would be to open the floodgates of feeling. And to do that would return poetry to its primal source, for, in the preface's most famous phrase, 'all good poetry is the spontaneous overflow of powerful feelings'.

Wordsworth's aim was to root out all 'falsehood of description' and to escape received 'poetic diction' – the tendency of 18th-century verse to turn 'fish' into 'the finny tribe'. The language of good poetry is no different from that of good prose, claimed Wordsworth: the gaudy phraseology and figures of speech traditionally associated with poetry choke what John Keats, in one of his rich epistolary reflections on creativity, was soon to call 'the true voice of feeling'.

'I have at all times endeavoured to look steadily at my subject', wrote Wordsworth in the preface. What he discovered from his steady gaze on death and loss and pain was that sincerity needs simplicity. Among the most peculiarly haunting of the 1798 *Lyrical Ballads* is 'The Idiot Boy'. This must be the first poem in any language on the subject of a Down's syndrome child. It is at once touching, funny, and just a little holy. It says something about the special grace of both handicapped children and those who care for them. Its particular brand of sincerity was new to poetry.

The word 'Romanticism' conjures up an idea of the artist alone in his garret, writing in a frenzy of inspiration, as suggested by an image in the memoirs of the composer Hector Berlioz: 'I was finishing my cantata when the Revolution broke out . . . I dashed off the final pages of my orchestral score to the sound of stray bullets . . . pattering on the wall outside my window.' The Romantic is defined on the one hand by solitude and on the other by a backdrop of political turmoil. Having finished his cantata, Berlioz goes out to join the revolutionary throng, but somehow he is never just one of the crowd.

One moment Wordsworth is wandering 'lonely as a cloud' as daffodils bob in the wind beside Ullswater, the next he is in Paris in the eye of the revolutionary storm, proclaiming what bliss it was 'in that dawn to be alive'. But Romantic solitude was often an illusion, a poetic device. Wordsworth didn't wander alone: he was accompanied by his sister Dorothy and it was she who observed the movement of the daffodils. Wordsworth's poem was written in retrospect, out of what he called, in another key phrase from the preface to *Lyrical Ballads*, 'emotion recollected in tranquillity'. It was inspired as much by his sister's journal as by the original walk.

English Romantic poetry was a deeply collaborative phenomenon. Its first wave, in the 1790s, was associated with the 'Lake School' (Wordsworth, Coleridge, and Robert Southey), its second, during the Regency, with the 'Satanic School' (Lord Byron and the Shelleys) and the 'Cockney School' (Keats, Leigh Hunt, William Hazlitt, and Charles Lamb). Though hostile, conservative critics attached the labels, the sense of collective endeavour among the groupings was pervasive. Several of the key manifestos for the new poetry – *Lyrical Ballads*, Hazlitt and Leigh Hunt's essay collection *The Round Table* (1817) – were jointly written. Mary Shelley edited her husband Percy's poems for publication, and he provided a preface for her novel *Frankenstein*. Some of the great solo-authored works were the product of creative dialogue: Wordsworth's epic autobiographical poem, known posthumously as *The Prelude* (published 1850), was conceived as a meditation addressed to Coleridge; Wordsworth in turn contributed a key stanza to Coleridge's most famous poem, 'The Ancient Mariner'. Even the 'Northamptonshire Peasant Poet' John Clare, a solitary-seeming figure if ever there was one, relied on his better-educated friends to help him polish his work.

Modernism

A revolution in poetic diction and a collective literary endeavour with its aims encapsulated in a series of manifestos: these were also characteristics of the 'Modernist' revolution of the early 20th century.

In the autumn of 1912, the American poet Ezra Pound met in the tearoom of the British Museum with his former fiancée Hilda Doolittle and the young English writer Richard Aldington. All three were keen to strip English poetry of the florid excesses into which late Romanticism had sunk. They had found new models in ancient Chinese, Japanese, and Greek lyric poetry, and in the example of modern French Symbolist verse, which had recently been championed in a powerful essay by another member of their circle, the working-class auto-didact F. S. Flint, who had extolled the virtues of free verse and concentrated imagery.

Pound was acting on behalf of the Chicago magazine *Poetry*. He read some of Doolittle's lapidary neo-Greek lyrics, signed them 'H. D. "Imagiste"' (the pared-down initials themselves an emblem of Imagist minimalism), and dispatched them to Harriet Monroe, the editor in Chicago. Examples of both H. D.'s work and Aldington's were soon in print in *Poetry*. The April 1913 issue included Pound's own 'In a station of the metro', which compacts into its two lines a suggestion of Japanese art, the ghosts of the classical underworld, and the modern city commuter, the elements of the image spaced on the page as a gesture towards Chinese ideograms:

> The apparition   of these faces   in the crowd :
> Petals   on a wet, black   bough .

A formal manifesto for the Imagist movement had appeared in the previous month's issue. Though drafted by Pound, it appeared under Flint's name (they later argued over their debt both to each other and to T. E. Hulme, another member of the group):

1) Direct treatment of the 'thing' whether subjective or objective.
2) To use absolutely no word that does not contribute to the presentation.
3) As regarding rhythm: to compose in the sequence of the musical phrase, not in sequence of a metronome.

'An "Image" is that which presents an intellectual and emotional complex in an instant of time', Pound added in a companion piece called 'A Few Don'ts for an Imagiste':

> It is the presentation of such a 'complex' instantaneously which gives that sense of sudden liberation; that sense of freedom from time limits and space limits; that sense of sudden growth, which we

experience in the presence of the greatest works of art. It is better to present one Image in a lifetime than to produce Voluminous works.

Fracture, fragmentation, disruption of temporal sequence, a stripping away of old decorums and elaborations: these signs of modern times were magnified by the Great War, which cast its shadow over almost everything written in the 1920s. T. S. Eliot's *The Waste Land* (1922), the central text in the repertoire of Modernist poetry – the draft was revised by Pound – is a heap of broken images, a collection of fragments shored against the ruin of the post-war world, a Babel of voices dramatizing the nervous breakdown of a poet and an age. Yet it is also an act of homage to the long tradition of Western poetry, written in accordance with Pound's prescription 'Be influenced by as many great artists as you can, but have the decency either to acknowledge the debt outright, or to try to conceal it'.

It was only in the late 1920s that the term 'Modernist' was applied to Imagism and its successor movements such as the 'Vorticism' promulgated by the irascible Wyndham Lewis during the war. The context was a critique written by two other poets, Robert Graves and Laura Riding. H. D. had made a virtue of the fact that the work of the foundational lyric poet of ancient Greece, Sappho, only survived in the form of fragments. Because a fragment was incomplete, obscure, evocative but elusive, it was regarded as somehow more beautiful than a complete poem. Pound took this idea to an extreme in the fragmentary lyric 'Papyrus', published in his collection *Lustra* (1916). Graves and Riding were not impressed:

When modernist poetry or what, not so long ago, passed for modernist poetry, can reach the stage where the following:

> Papyrus
> Spring … …
> Too long … … …
> Gongula … … …

is seriously offered as a poem, there is some justification for the plain reader and orthodox critic who are frightened away from anything which may be labeled 'modernist' either in terms of condemnation or approbation. Who or what is Gongula? Is it a name of a person? of a town? of a musical instrument? Or is it the obsolete botanical word meaning 'spores'? Or is it a mistake for Gongora, the Spanish poet from whom the word 'gongorism' is formed, meaning 'an affected elegance of style, also called "cultism"'? And why 'Papyrus'? ... Rather than answer any of these questions and be driven to the shame-faced bluff of making much out of little, the common-sense reader retires to surer ground.

(Robert Graves and Laura Riding, *A Survey of Modernist Poetry*, 1927)

The Imagists had reacted against the lushness of late Romantic, predominantly rural, 'Georgian' poetry. Graves and Riding in turn reacted against them. Graves in particular proclaimed allegiance instead to a tradition of honest English emotion that he found exemplified in the poetry of Thomas Hardy. For the rest of the 20th century, English poetry was engaged in a battle between Hardy's 'true voice of feeling' and the Modernist commitment to difficulty and experimentation.

Chapter 6
Among the English poets

The poet as laureate

The modern experience of literature is predominantly silent and solitary. This has not always been the case. The ancient bards did not write their poems down; they memorized and recited their narratives. In *The Canterbury Tales*, poems are shared stories to enliven a journey. The romance of *Sir Gawain and the Green Knight* is set during a Christmas feast in order to perform its own role as a tale to pass away a long winter's evening. George Herbert and William Blake sang their own poems.

Dramatic poetry is by its nature aural and communal. Lyric poetry in its earliest forms was sung competitively. In ancient Greece, winning poets (like winning athletes) were crowned with wreaths of laurel, a plant sacred to Apollo, the god of poetry. This is the origin of the term 'laureate'. Among the original kinds of lyric poetry were the ode, which was a poem of praise, and the elegy, which was a poem of mourning and memory. By writing odes and elegies, poets could win patronage, which remained the only way of supporting their art before the emergence of a genuine literary marketplace in the 18th century.

Shakespeare became rich on the proceeds not of his poetry but of his shareholding in a commercial theatre company. No English poet found wealth from the publishing trade until 1714, when Alexander Pope secured an unprecedented deal with the publisher Bernard Lintot to translate Homer's *Iliad* in six volumes at the rate of 200 guineas per volume. He also secured 750 free copies for subscribers, enabling him to pocket the guinea per head that they paid up front. Calculating via the retail price index, these earnings amount to nearly 200,000 pounds in today's terms, while using an average earnings index the early 21st-century equivalent is in excess of two million pounds. Pope spent a goodly proportion of the proceeds on a handsome villa at Twickenham and the design of an elaborate garden there.

Edmund Spenser's epic romance *The Faerie Queene* (1590–6) came to be regarded as the first English national epic. Spenser drew upon native Arthurian material and, with the syncretic art that was the peculiar excellence of the Elizabethans, overlaid it with classical influences (the magical transformations of Ovid as much as the sterner matter of Virgil), with the romantic entanglements of Renaissance Italian epic (notably Ariosto's *Orlando Furioso*), and with his own brand of invention. Newly minted knights stand in for Lancelot, Gawain, and the rest: the Red Cross Knight, a distinctively Protestant version of St George; Sir Guyon, struggling to maintain the virtue of temperance as he encounters an alluring temptress called Acrasia in a Bower of Bliss; Britomart, a cross-dressed female warrior intended to be particularly flattering to Queen Elizabeth; then there is Artegall, seeker after justice, who is accompanied by a flail-wielding iron man called Talus, suggestive of an uncompromising approach to rebellion in Ireland; Sir Calidore, who discovers courtesy in a pastoral world; while Arthur himself rides in to offer assistance at moments of crisis. Spenser earned little from the poem's publication, but the enterprise won him a pension from Queen Elizabeth I.

Like Chaucer and John Skelton (Henry VIII's tutor) before him, then Ben Jonson and William Davenant after him, Spenser was an unofficial Poet Laureate. The role first became an official royal office in 1668, when the deeply cultured King Charles II conferred the title on John Dryden, who had ingratiated himself at court the previous year with the publication of *Annus mirabilis: the Year of Wonders, MDCLXVI*, a heroic poem about two events in 1666 that Puritan oppositional voices had represented as signs of divine displeasure at Charles's government and morals: the second Anglo-Dutch War, which had seen an enemy fleet sail up the River Medway, and the Great Fire of London. Dryden's riposte was to see a divine pattern of miraculous salvation from a much worse outcome and to portray the king himself going heroically into the city to help put out the fire.

Dryden converted to Roman Catholicism in 1685, which was convenient, since that was the year when Charles II was succeeded by his openly Catholic brother James II. With the Glorious Revolution of 1688, and the arrival of the Protestant monarchs William and Mary, Dryden lost his office to the Whig poet and playwright Thomas Shadwell, the first of the long line of Laureates to be mocked in later generations as second-rate placemen. Dryden had already lampooned him in *Mac Flecknoe: A Satyr upon the Trew-Blue-Protestant Poet T. S.* (1682); in Alexander Pope's mock epic compendium of bad writers, *The Dunciad*, he is 'Sh**well'.

Romanticism's emphasis on the writer's own feelings, as exemplified by William Wordsworth's decision to create an epic poem not about British history or the war in heaven, but about the growth of his own mind, was in effect a privatizing of poetry. Keats wrote odes not to monarchs and prospective patrons, but to a Grecian urn, to the mood of melancholy, to a nightingale, and to the season of autumn. If the poet did have a public role, it was to be as a prophet crying in the wilderness (Blake and Shelley saw themselves in these terms), not as official spokesman for monarch and nation. That is why in 1813 the younger Romantics such as Byron and Hazlitt greeted with dismay the acceptance of the Laureateship by Robert Southey, sometime apologist for the French Revolution and companion of Coleridge in a fanciful scheme to establish a Utopian community of free love on the banks of the Susquehanna River.

Alfred Lord Tennyson restored a degree of dignity to the office of Poet Laureate, in that his voice seemed to articulate the mood of his age. Four years after becoming Laureate on Wordsworth's death, he read an account in *The Times* newspaper of the disastrous Charge of the Light Brigade during the Battle of Balaclava in the Crimea. Within minutes, he had dashed out a poem in a galloping dactylic rhythm: 'Half a league, half a league' – stress, unstress, unstress; stress, unstress, unstress – 'Half a league onward',

> All in the valley of Death
>> Rode the six hundred.
> 'Forward, the Light Brigade!
> Charge for the guns!' he said:
> Into the valley of Death
>> Rode the six hundred.

The poem is at once critical of the high command ('Someone had blundered') and uplifting in praise of the courage of the horsemen. Like many memorable English poems that confront mortality, it draws allusively on the twenty-third Psalm, in the 1611 translation of the Bible: 'Yea, though I walk through the valley of the shadow of death, I will fear no evil: For thou art with me.'

For Tennyson, though, such public poems were of far less importance than his lyrics of private grief, such as the sustained elegiac sequence *In Memoriam A. H. H.* (1850), a cumulative assembly of lyrics that became a quasi-epic interior journey. 'The Charge of the Light Brigade' was a popular hit, but thoughtful Victorian readers in times of darkness found deeper value in the aching quatrains of the requiem for Tennyson's beloved Arthur Hallam. 'Next to the Bible, *In Memoriam* is my comfort', said Queen Victoria after the death of Prince Albert.

Modern lyric verse is often a vehicle for poets' quarrels with themselves (Yeats's phrase, eminently applicable to Ted Hughes and Geoffrey Hill) or for 'the relief of a personal and wholly insignificant grouse against life' (Eliot's self-deprecatory characterization of *The Waste Land*, which might have served Philip Larkin as a motto). On the rare occasions when serious, high-quality public verse does appear, it is often angry, disillusioned, written from the standpoint of the outsider or in sympathy with the dispossessed. Tony Harrison's 'V', written in the wake of the 1984–5 miners' strike, is a fine example. Modern poets have accordingly not been inclined to welcome the public burden of the Laureateship.

The pity of war

There's been an elegiac tinge to the air of this country ever since the end of the Great War.

(Geoffrey Hill, 1981)

Just occasionally, it is still possible for a poet to speak on behalf of the nation. One of Carol Ann Duffy's first poems on becoming the first female Poet Laureate in 2009 was a moving elegy on the deaths of Henry Allingham and Harry Patch, the last two fighting 'Tommies' of the First World War. Entitled 'Last Post' (readily available online), it begins with a quotation from Wilfred Owen's 'Strange Meeting' ('In all my dreams, before my helpless sight, / He plunges at me, guttering, choking, drowning'), then proceeds to imagine the war dead – 'Harry, Tommy, Wilfred, Edward, Bert' – coming back to life 'crammed with love, work, children, talent, English beer, good food'. The poem ends

You see the poet tuck away his pocket-book and smile.
If poetry could truly tell it backwards,
then it would.

Duffy's controlling image is of a film reel being rewound. We remember grainy black-and-white footage of soldier boys going over the top and being mown down like grass in a meadow. Imagine them getting back up again. What if they had survived: if English poetry had not lost 'Wilfred' (Owen) and 'Edward' (Thomas)? But the poets *have* survived, through their readers, whereas most of the fallen are remembered only by their families and on gravestones or war memorials. Poetry *can* truly tell it backwards, by looking backwards and honouring its own alumni.

Duffy's first stanza includes a further allusion to Wilfred Owen ('Dulce – No – Decorum – No – Pro patria mori'). Her second stanza names the dead poets and nods to a fellow writer's approach to the Great War through the poignancy of its suffering horses: sometime Children's Laureate Michael Morpurgo's *War Horse* was being staged in a triumphant National Theatre adaptation as Duffy wrote. And in the last stanza, she seems to allude to the pocket-book found on Edward Thomas's body, intact, but creased by the shell blast, after he fell near Arras in April 1917. Her words reel the voices of the past back into life.

Poetry as dialogue with the dead: *'Dulce et decorum est'* winds the reel back further still. Owen's title alludes bitterly to a much-quoted line from an ode by Horace: *dulce et decorum est pro patria mori* ('it is sweet and right to die for your country'). An examination of the original holograph manuscript brings other poets into the dialogue. Here we may see not only Owen's own careful revisions ('gargling', 'gurgling', 'goggling', 'guttering', for the soldier drowning in the gas attack), but also markings by his fellow poet Siegfried Sassoon, who helped him to perfect his art when they were convalescing from shell shock at Craiglockhart War Hospital. And from the original titles, 'To Jessie Pope etc.' and 'To a certain poetess', it becomes apparent that Owen is aiming his fire less at Horace than at modern apologists for 'the old lie'. Jessie Pope was one of the gung-ho patriot poets who regularly published lines such as the following in the *Daily Mail*, exhorting young men to join up and go to their deaths in the mud of Flanders:

Dulce et Decorum est.

To ~~Jessie Pope etc.~~ To a certain Poetess

Bent double, like old beggars under sacks,
Knock-kneed, coughing like hags, we cursed through sludge,
Till on the ~~haunting~~ flares we turned our backs,
And towards our distant rest began to trudge.
Dead slow we moved. Many had lost their boots,
But limped on, blood-shod. All went lame; all blind;
Drunk with fatigue; deaf even to the hoots
~~Of disappointed shells that dropped behind.~~
Of ~~tired-voiced~~ five-nines that dropped behind.
~~two, outstripped~~

Then somewhere near in front: Whew... fup... fop... fup...
Gas-shells or duds? We loosened masks, in case —
And listened.... Nothing... Far rumouring of Krupp;..
Then ~~smashed,~~ stinging poison hit us in the face,
Gas! GAS! ~~An ecstasy of~~ Quick, boys! — An ecstasy of fumbling.
Fitting the clumsy helmets just in time.
But someone still was yelling out, and stumbling,
And floundering like a man in fire or lime. —
Dim, through the misty panes and thick green light,
As under a dark sea, I saw him drowning.

In all my dreams, before my helpless sight,
He plunges at me, ~~gargling,~~ choking, drowning.
~~gurgling~~
~~goggling~~
guttering

4. 'Dulce et decorum est': original manuscript in the hand of Wilfred Owen, with the poet's own revisions and further suggestions by Siegfried Sassoon

Who's for the game, the biggest that's played,
The red crashing game of a fight? ...
Who'll toe the line for the signal to 'Go!'?
Who'll give his country a hand?
Who wants a turn to himself in the show?

And who wants a seat in the stand?
Who knows it won't be a picnic – not much –
Yet eagerly shoulders a gun?
Who would much rather come back with a crutch
Than lie low and be out of the fun?

'Never such innocence again', as Philip Larkin wrote of the men in cloth caps in long uneven lines, waiting to sign on for king and country in 1914, 'Grinning as if it were all / An August Bank Holiday lark' ('MCMXIV', in *The Whitsun Weddings*, 1964).

What is poetry for in time of war? Owen famously wrote 'Above all I am not concerned with Poetry. My subject is War, and the pity of War. The Poetry is in the Pity.' He and Sassoon and Isaac Rosenberg angrily and sadly told what it was really like in the trenches, and made it impossible for anyone thereafter to say *dulce et decorum est* without irony or reservation. In some respects, they shaped war poetry so decisively that it was impossible to go beyond them – though Keith Douglas made a very honourable attempt in the Second World War.

For soldiers themselves, poetry can be a solace, as Tennyson's *In Memoriam* was to Queen Victoria. Many a knapsack on the Western Front contained a copy of A. E. Housman's elegiac *A Shropshire Lad* (1896). Poetry could offer a more subtle form of patriotism than that of Jessie Pope. When Edward Thomas, writer of lush rural prose, was asked why he had decided to join the Artists' Rifles, he bent down, picked up a pinch of English earth, and said 'For this'. The war made him into a poet. The image of England for which many imagined they were fighting was conjured up in a recruitment poster, sponsored by the London Underground, which juxtaposed a country churchyard with some lines about rural ease by the Romantic poet Samuel Rogers.

The Underground Railways of London, knowing how many of their passengers are now engaged on important business in France and other parts of the world, send out this reminder of home. Thanks are due to George Clausen R.A. for the drawing.

A WISH. Mine be a cot beside the hill; The swallow oft beneath my thatch Around my ivied porch shall spring The village church among the trees
A bee-hive's hum shall soothe my ear; Shall twitter from her clay-built nest; Each fragrant flower that drinks the dew, Where first our marriage-vows were given,
A willowy brook that turns a mill, Oft shall the pilgrim lift the latch, And Lucy at her wheel shall sing With merry peals shall swell the breeze
With many a fall shall linger near. And share my meal, a welcome guest. In russet gown and apron blue. And point with taper spire to Heaven.

5. 'A Wish': First World War recruitment poster, with image by George Clausen and rural poem by Romantic poet Samuel Rogers

In the Armageddon of war, the rhythms of rural life can provide an image of stability and endurance. Edward Thomas meditates along these lines, without jingoism or didacticism, in 'As the team's head-brass' (1916): 'I watched the clods crumble and topple over / After the ploughshare and the stumbling team.' Thomas Hardy follows a similar track when writing 'In Time of "the Breaking of Nations"' (1916, the title alluding to the Old Testament prophet Jeremiah, 'Thou art my battle axe and weapons of war: for with thee will I break in pieces the nations'):

> Only a man harrowing clods
> In a slow silent walk
> With an old horse that stumbles and nods
> Half asleep as they stalk.

The poetry of desire: John Donne

> Only two topics can be of the least interest to a serious and studious mind: sex and the dead.
>
> (W. B. Yeats, 1927)

There are two kinds of elegy. One is the poem in memory of the dead, such as John Milton's 'Lycidas'. An elegy may commemorate a particular person or may be a more general meditation on loss and mortality, of which the most celebrated example is Thomas Gray's 'Elegy written in a Country Churchyard' (1751), written in five-beat (iambic pentameter) quatrains as assured as any in the language, 'The cúrfew tólls the knéll of párting dáy ... The páths of glóry léad but tó the gráve'. Elegies on the deaths of fellow poets and loved ones have been one of the richest strains in English lyric poetry. The line of elegies on poets extends from the Earl of Surrey remembering Thomas Wyatt in the 16th century, to Thomas Carew remembering Donne in the 17th, to Shelley on Keats in the 19th (*Adonais*), to Auden on Yeats in the 20th. Elegies on loved ones include Ben Jonson's beautiful little poem calling his lost son his 'best piece of poetry', to Henry King's 'exequy' on his wife (1620s), to Hardy remembering his ('Poems of 1912–13'), to Douglas Dunn (*Elegies*, 1985), Ted Hughes (*Birthday Letters*, 1998), and Christopher Reid (*A Scattering*, 2009) in recent times.

The other kind of elegy is a love poem. The term 'elegiac' originally referred to a classical poetic metre that was often used to convey mournful matter; the Roman lyric poets Catullus, Propertius, and Ovid frequently employed it in their love poetry. So it was that when Christopher Marlowe translated Ovid's *Amores*, he called them *Ovid's Elegies*. When we are in love, we reach for poetry: well-written verse heightens and intensifies the language of emotion in heart-racing rhythms, while its metaphors open the eyes to new horizons, and its rhymes bring words together as if they were kisses. It is no surprise that the Ovidian poetry of sexual desire is a strand woven through English Literature, running from Shakespeare's *Venus and Adonis* (1593), through Keats's 'The Eve of St Agnes' (1820), to Christina Rossetti's *Goblin Market* (1862), and beyond.

In the 1590s, the elegy became almost as popular a form as the sonnet for the display of the art of love. It is in one of John Donne's elegies that we find his gorgeously erotic exploration of a lover's body:

> Licence my roving hands, and let them go,
> Before, behind, between, above, below.
> O my America! my new-found-land,
> My kingdom, safeliest when with one man man'd,
> My mine of precious stone: my Empery,
> How blest am I in thus discovering thee!
> To enter in these bonds, is to be free;
> Then, where my hand is set, my seal shall be.

> Full nakedness! All joys are due to thee,
> As souls unbodied, bodies uncloth'd must be
> To taste whole joys.

('To his mistress going to bed')

Donne catches the moment of the lover's experience in all its intensity, then leaps to reflect upon it, and philosophize around it, with extraordinary ingenuity and complexity. As Dr Johnson said of Donne's disciple Abraham Cowley, who wrote a poem comparing a lover's heart to a hand grenade, 'the most heterogeneous ideas are yoked by violence together'.

Shakespeare was the most impersonal of poets: even after four centuries, no one has unpacked the personal experiences – if indeed there were any – behind his sonnets. Donne, by contrast, conveys a sense of personality throughout his work. He was indeed the first major author in the language to make poetry out of his own life. Not until Wordsworth and the Romantics two centuries later would other poets make themselves the principal subject of their writing in such a sustained way. Donne was also the first literary man to write intimate and personal letters that have survived. He was the subject of one of the earliest biographies in the language, written very soon after his death by Izaak Walton. The dramatic reversals that marked his life made him an ideal subject.

He was born into a recusant family in 1573: his mother was a descendant of no less a figure than the martyred Sir Thomas More. His brother would die in prison after being arrested for harbouring a Catholic priest. Donne himself went to Oxford University at the age of twelve not because he was precociously intellectual (although he was), but so that he could complete his degree before the age of sixteen, when he would have had to subscribe to the Oath of Allegiance to the Anglican Church and Queen. In his twenties, he succeeded in distancing himself from his Catholic origins sufficiently to gain the post of private secretary to Sir Thomas

Egerton, the Lord Keeper. But then he fell in love with his master's teenage niece and secretly married her, a union that cost him his job. The marriage, though, turned out to be long and happy, which is a little surprising in view of the unashamed philandering of Donne's youth. Despite his inauspicious beginning, Donne ended his life as Dean of St Paul's Cathedral and the most famous preacher of the day. His sermons attracted crowds as large and rapturous as those who attended Shakespeare's plays.

Most of his verse was written for a circle of friends and patrons, very little of it being published in his lifetime. In the close-knit world of genteel Elizabethan society, word soon spread that he was a major new talent. His most admired poems were 'The Calm' and 'The Storm', a dazzling diptych inspired by his marauding maritime adventures to Cadiz and the Azores in the service of the charismatic Earl of Essex. His satires, emerging from his time as a trainee lawyer in the Inns of Courts, painted excoriating pictures of contemporary London, but also wrestled in his close-packed rhyming couplets with the pursuit of spiritual wisdom and the work of religious devotion:

> in strange way
> To stand inquiring right, is not to stray;
> To sleep, or run wrong, is. On a huge hill,
> Cragg'd and steep, Truth stands, and he that will
> Reach her, about must, and about must go;
> And what the hill's suddenness resists, win so;
> Yet strive so, that before age, death's twilight,
> Thy Soul rest, for none can work in that night.
>
> (Satire 3)

His *Songs and Sonnets* are the most forceful love poems in the language. Their immediacy comes above all from the sense of a voice speaking directly to the lover with whom he is sharing a bed while also inviting in the overhearing reader: 'I wonder by my troth what thou and I / Did till we loved?' ('The Good Morrow'); 'For God's sake,

hold your tongue and let me love' ('The Canonization'); 'Twice or thrice
had I loved thee, / Before I knew thy face or name' ('Air and Angels').

Ben Jonson said that Donne wrote all his best poetry before the age
of twenty-five. Donne himself made a distinction between his
youthful 'Jack the lad' persona and the venerable figure of
Dr Donne of St Paul's. Yet the religious poetry to which he turned
in the second half of his life – and indeed the language of his
sermons – retains the passion, and indeed some of the eroticism,
of the early work. Now, though, instead of him seducing a
mistress, it is a case of God ravishing him:

> Batter my heart, three-person'd God...
> Take me to you, imprison me, for I
> Except you'enthrall me, never shall be free,
> Nor ever chaste, except you ravish me.
>
> (*Holy Sonnet* 10)

Donne refuses to separate out the experiences of his senses and his
spirit. No writer answers more rigorously to Coleridge's demand
that being a poet means bringing 'the whole soul of man into
activity'. His prose meditations on death are as rich in metaphor as
his poetic anatomies of love:

> No man is an island, entire of itself; every man is a piece of
> the continent, a part of the main ... any man's death diminishes
> me, because I am involved in mankind, and therefore never send
> to know for whom the bells tolls; it tolls for thee.
>
> (*Devotions upon Emergent Occasions*, XVII)

On the faultlines between Catholicism and Protestantism,
theological scholasticism and the 'new philosophy' of universal
scepticism, in search of a public role but committed to the integrity
of the private self, Donne embodies literature's power to straddle
past and present, history and eternity.

Chapter 7
Shakespeare and dramatic literature

'See it feelingly'

On to the stage walks an actor playing the part of a fugitive aristocrat dressed as a peasant, leading another actor playing the part of an old nobleman whose eyes have been plucked out on stage earlier in the play. They are pretending to walk up a hill. 'You do climb it now', says the man disguised as the peasant, 'Look how we labour'. 'Methinks the ground is even', replies the old man, who does not know that the supposed peasant is really his son. The audience has sight like the young man, but what they see is a flat surface (the stage), which is what the old man senses. Only in the imagination is the ascent 'Horrible steep'. 'Hark, do you hear the sea?' the young man then asks. 'No, truly', says the blind man. Again, it is the blind man who speaks of the reality in the theatre where the play was first staged – there was no sound system or recorded effect. Those modern stage and film directors who introduce the sound of the sea at this point are misreading the stagecraft.

The young man says that the old man's failure to hear the sea shows that his 'other senses grow imperfect / By your eyes' anguish'. The old man agrees: something must have happened to his hearing, because the young man's voice is altered. When they first met, he spoke in the voice of Poor Tom, a lunatic fugitive beggar; now he is 'better spoken'. In one way, that is the truth: his linguistic register has changed. But in another way, it is not true: he is still the old man's noble son in disguise. 'You're much deceived; in nothing am I changed / But in my garments.' The old man could not have seen the change of costume, but the theatre audience will have registered it.

The young man, whose real name is Edgar, tells the old man, who is the Earl of Gloucester, to stand still. He then conjures up a mental picture of the view from a cliff top. In an earlier scene, we have learned that they are on their way to Dover (where Shakespeare's acting company had played when on tour), so we are to imagine that we are on the top of the white cliffs, above the English Channel. In the 18th century, the highest of them was named Shakespeare's Cliff, in honour of this speech:

> How fearful
> And dizzy 'tis to cast one's eyes so low!
> The crows and choughs that wing the midway air
> Show scarce so gross as beetles: half way down
> Hangs one that gathers samphire, dreadful trade!
> Methinks he seems no bigger than his head.
> The fishermen that walk upon the beach
> Appear like mice, and yond tall anchoring bark
> Diminished to her cock, her cock, a buoy
> Almost too small for sight. The murmuring surge,
> That on th'unnumbered idle pebble chafes,
> Cannot be heard so high. I'll look no more,
> Lest my brain turn and the deficient sight
> Topple down headlong.

The scene is written in blank verse and the movement of the poetry is contrived to evoke the sense of hanging on the edge of a precipice. 'Half way down' – pause for the line ending – 'Hangs one that gathers samphire'. The scene is painted according to the laws of perspective: the further the distance, the smaller the object. By the end of the speech, Edgar has conceded that the sea cannot really be heard and the progression from 'too small for sight' to 'the deficient sight' has somehow put him in the position of his blind father. They then change places, with Gloucester saying 'Set me where you stand'. Edgar stands aside and tells the audience that he is trifling with his father's suicidal despair in order to cure it. Gloucester then addresses the gods, renounces the world, and topples down headlong in attempted suicide. Not, of course, over a cliff, but simply onto the even ground of the stage.

Edgar then transforms both himself and the scene. He pretends to be a man on the beach below, helping the old man to his feet and telling him that he has miraculously survived the mighty fall. The supposed miracle persuades Gloucester that he must stoically bear his affliction rather than commit the moral crime of suicide.

At this point, another actor comes on, playing the part of a mad king wearing a crown of weeds. The dialogue again turns on the recognition or misrecognition of voices: 'I know that voice', 'The trick of that voice I do well remember'. The mad king, whose name is Lear, variously mistakes the old blind man for his own daughter ('with a white beard') and a man who is on trial for adultery (which Gloucester has in fact committed – the play began with him introducing his illegitimate son Edmund to the court). Eventually, the madman registers the other's blindness, but says that it is no impediment to an understanding of the world's injustice:

> **LEAR** O, ho, are you there with me? No eyes in your head, nor no money in your purse? Your eyes are in a heavy case, your purse in a light, yet you see how this world goes.
>
> **GLOUCESTER** I see it feelingly.
>
> **LEAR** What, art mad? A man may see how this world goes with no eyes. Look with thine ears: see how yond justice rails upon yond simple thief. Hark, in thine ear: change places, and handy-dandy, which is the justice, which is the thief? Thou hast seen a farmer's dog bark at a beggar?

GLOUCESTER Ay, sir.

LEAR And the creature run from the cur? There thou mightst behold
the great image of authority: a dog's obeyed in office.

Authority is seen to derive from the trappings of power – the robes
of a judge, the bark of a dog – and not from a natural or divine
order. This exchange was played out, without censorship, on a
platform stage in the banqueting hall at Whitehall on the day
after Christmas in 1606, before His Majesty King James I and VI of
England and Scotland. A little later in the scene, King Lear
takes on the part of a preacher moralizing to the effect that
'When we are born we cry that we are come / To this great stage
of fools'. For much of the play, the stage has indeed been peopled
by fools of various kinds. It has been the fools, not the self-serving
courtiers, who have spoken with honesty, truth, and wisdom at
peril of their lives or their sanity.

In the remainder of the scene, Edgar plays further parts: a man
of sufficient gentility to be addressed as 'Sir', a poor man offering
pity, a countryman speaking in dialect ('And 'ch'ud ha' been
zwaggered out of my life, 'twould not ha' been zo long as 'tis by a
vortnight'). He ends the scene as he begins it, leading the old
man away. Poignantly, he calls him 'father', though still without
acknowledging that he really is Gloucester's son.

Theatre is made by pretending. The actor playing Edgar pretends
to 'labour' in his walk in order to suggest uphill motion. He puts
on different voices, different costumes. The actor playing Gloucester
pretends to be blind, pretends to be a man who believes he is
committing suicide by jumping off a cliff. The actor playing Lear
pretends to be mad but also to be wise, pretends not to recognize
Gloucester. The men and women backstage who have sewn the
costumes and fashioned the crown of weeds have played their
part in the pretence. Throughout a scene such as this, which occurs
in the fourth act of *King Lear*, Shakespeare not only deploys a

highly complicated, many-layered stagecraft, he also reflects self-consciously upon the nature of theatre. When we ask who these people really are and at what level they are 'playing', we enter into a mental spiral as vertiginous as Edgar's visual cliff fall. We find ourselves in several places at once: the theatre, the ancient British world within the play, the monarchical world in which Shakespeare wrote, and our own sense of 'how this world goes'. We take the point that the world is a stage of fools, but at the same time we sense that the feigned preacher's voice is mocking this idea as a cliché.

Shakespeare always seems to be one step ahead of us. Throughout *King Lear*, characters who think they have made sense of the world find themselves being mocked by the next turn of events. In the closing scene, the Duke of Albany tries to orchestrate the ending, to make order out of chaos, but each of his resolutions is followed by new disaster: he greets the restored Edgar, then immediately hears the news of Gloucester's death, then the news of Goneril's and Regan's violent deaths; then in response to the news that Cordelia is to be hanged, Albany says 'The gods defend her', only for Lear to enter with her in his arms already hanged. The gods have not defended her. Then Albany tries to give power back to Lear – who promptly dies. Then he tries to persuade Kent and Edgar to divide the kingdom, but Kent gracefully goes off to die. Yet through all this, the human bonds shine through. The emotions enacted on stage evoke an emotional response in the audience. Like Gloucester, we 'see it feelingly'. At the end, we don't really have any answers to the big questions that the play has asked, such as 'is there any cause in nature that make these hard hearts?', but we have learned the value of speaking 'what we feel, not what we ought to say'.

Seeing versus reading

In *The Tatler* (1709), Joseph Addison singled out Edgar's description of Dover Cliff for high praise: 'He who can read it without being giddy has a very good head, or a very bad one.' Dr Samuel Johnson begged to differ: 'It should be all precipice, – all vacuum', he told Boswell,

> The crows impede your fall. The diminished appearance of the boats, and other circumstances, are all very good description; but do not impress the mind at once with the horrible idea of immense height. The impression is divided; you pass on by computation, from one stage of the tremendous space to another.

Literary criticism has always involved debates of this kind regarding the success or failure of particular pieces of writing. Dissenting voices such as Johnson's are valuable antidotes to complacent pleasantries about Shakespeare's infallible genius.

Johnson did, however, grant that 'there is perhaps no play which keeps the attention so strongly fixed' as *King Lear*, no play 'which so much agitates our passions ... So powerful is the current of the poet's imagination, that the mind, which once ventures within it, is hurried irresistibly along.' More than any other playwright, Shakespeare seems able to take the mind of his listener into that of his speaker. 'While we read it, we see not Lear, but we are Lear', wrote Charles Lamb a generation after Johnson. For Lamb, though, the experience of imaginative empathy with the mind of a Lear or a Hamlet could only be fully achieved in the experience of *reading*. Watching a play in the theatre was a poor substitute:

> To see Lear acted, to see an old man tottering about the stage with a walking-stick, turned out of doors by his daughters in a rainy night, has nothing in it but what is painful and disgusting. We want to take him into shelter and relieve him. That is all the feeling which the acting of Lear ever produced in me. But the Lear of Shakespeare cannot be acted. The contemptible machinery by which they mimic the storm which he goes out in, is not more adequate to represent the horrors of the real elements, than any actor can be to

represent Lear: they might more easily propose to personate the Satan of Milton upon a stage, or one of Michael Angelo's terrible figures.

(Lamb, 'On the Tragedies of Shakspeare, considered with reference to their fitness for stage representation', 1811)

Our first reaction to Lamb's idea that Shakespearean tragedy cannot be acted is likely to be one of incredulity. The plays were written to be acted. They have provided the greatest actors with their greatest triumphs: from Shakespeare's intimate friend Richard Burbage, for whom the parts were originally written, to Thomas Betterton in the Restoration era, to David Garrick in the 18th century, Edmund Kean and Henry Irving in the 19th, John Gielgud and Laurence Olivier in the 20th, Paul Scofield and Ian McKellen more recently, there has been an unbroken succession of Hamlets and Lears who are the glory of the English stage. What is more, *Hamlet* and *King Lear* and Shakespeare's other plays are so steeped in self-conscious theatricality that they cry out to be *played* in order to realize their meaning – as witnessed by the cliff scene and by Hamlet's staging of a play within the play, and by Macbeth's allusion to the 'poor player / That struts and frets his hour upon the stage', Cleopatra's imagining of the squeaking actor who will 'boy' her 'greatness / I'th'posture of a whore', and a hundred other 'metadramatic' moments.

We might then make allowances for Lamb in the light of the deficiencies of the theatre in his time. Shakespeare wrote for a platform stage thrust with immediacy and vitality into the auditorium, with minimal scenery and scenic effects, whereas in the 18th and 19th centuries the theatres royal at Covent Garden and Drury Lane were cavernous structures in which a proscenium arch separated actor from audience, and the action was cluttered and impeded by elaborate scene changes and crowds of extras brought on in the name of spectacle. If Lamb could have time-travelled back to Shakespeare's own time, or forward to the invention of the intimate black box studio theatre, he might after all have seen a production that took him inside Lear's head.

Another factor is that Lamb would not have had the opportunity to see the play in its original form: for 150 years, from the Restoration to the early Victorian period, it was displaced from the English stage by Nahum Tate's decorous and romantic rewriting, in which there is no Fool and there is a happy ending when Cordelia marries Edgar.

If we were theatre practitioners, we might go to the opposite extreme from Lamb and claim that Shakespeare's plays should *always* be regarded as scripts for performance, not texts to be analysed in the study or the classroom. We might argue that the force-feeding of Shakespeare's demanding language to schoolchildren for the purposes of examination is positively destructive of the enjoyment and enlightenment that the plays offer in performance, when the momentum of the plot and the evolving relationships between the characters are so forceful that it does not matter if we find ourselves not entirely sure what is meant by such phrases as Hamlet's 'Against the which, a moiety competent / Was gagèd by our king', or the Fool's 'O, nuncle, court holy-water in a dry house is better than this rain-water out o'door'. We might say that theatre is drama *before it becomes literature*, that Shakespeare is most Shakespearean when actor and audience meet in the live, shared space of the playhouse. In support of this view, it might be argued that whereas Ben Jonson carefully prepared his plays for publication, taking out some of the comic diversions that were meant for performance alone, Shakespeare showed no interest in the immortalization of his drama in print. He was a working playwright, the first to have the position of in-house dramatist within a theatre company. He wrote for particular actors, particular stage spaces, particular audiences (public, private, and courtly). He would be astonished to discover that his scripts have been turned into literature and submitted to more interpretations – moral, psychological, formal, political, sociological, historical, philosophical, biographical – than any other writings in the history of the world with the exception of Holy Scripture.

Mr. WILLIAM
SHAKESPEARES
COMEDIES,
HISTORIES, &
TRAGEDIES.

Published according to the True Originall Copies.

Martin Droeshout sculpsit London

LONDON
Printed by Isaac Iaggard, and Ed. Blount. 1623.

6. Shakespeare becomes literature? Title page of the First Folio of 1623, establishing the generic division of comedies, histories, and tragedies

But the claim that Shakespeare was not a *literary* dramatist is contestable. His fellow actors John Hemmings and Henry Condell manifestly had his (posthumous) interests at heart when they turned the plays into a collection of literary works in handsome Folio format, complete with prefatory address exhorting purchasers to read him again and again.

Even before this, about half of Shakespeare's plays, predominantly tragedies and histories, had been made available to readers, sometimes in editions authorized by the acting company. The scripts of *Richard III*, *Hamlet*, and *King Lear* printed in Shakespeare's lifetime were too long to be played uncut in the two or three hours that were allowed for public performances on the London stage, so it is possible that they represent the dramatist's own reading texts, written in full knowledge that they would be cut and altered when realized on stage.

Judged by frequency of reprinting, the surest indicator of demand in the literary marketplace, Shakespeare's *Henry IV, Part One* (famous for the characters of Sir John Falstaff and Henry Hotspur) and *Richard III* (famous for its eponymous villain) were two of the three most widely read plays in his lifetime. The third was an anonymous pastoral comedy called *Mucedorus* (1598, revived with additions by Shakespeare's acting company in 1610). The most frequently reprinted long poem of the age was Shakespeare's youthful erotic masterpiece *Venus and Adonis*. Clearly, then, Shakespeare was *read* as well as performed in his own lifetime.

The First Folio was, however, of tremendous importance in turning Shakespeare into a literary classic. By dividing the plays into three genres – comedies, histories, and tragedies – Hemmings and Condell drew attention to his unique versatility. In Ben Jonson's poem of praise, prefaced to the volume, Shakespeare is lauded as the equal of the great dramatists of the classical world in both tragedy and comedy. He is then said to have surpassed his English predecessors: John Lyly, who had laid the foundations of

Elizabethan comedy in plays such as *Endimion* (1591) and
Gallathea (1592), delicate dramas of wit, combat, courtship, and
cross-dressing written for boy actors; Thomas Kyd, whose *Spanish
Tragedy* (1588) was the archetypal tragedy of bloody revenge; and
Christopher Marlowe, who pioneered the soaring line of blank
verse and the figure of the overreaching anti-hero – all-conquering
Tamburlaine, Machiavellian schemer Barabas the rich Jew of Malta,
and intellectually restless Dr John Faustus. Lyly did not write
tragedies; neither Marlowe nor Kyd seems to have excelled in
comedy. Ben Jonson was the other great comic dramatist of the
age – Coleridge regarded *The Alchemist* (1610) as one of the most
perfectly plotted literary works ever written – but he failed badly
in tragedy: *Sejanus His Fall* flopped when staged at the Globe in
1603. Shakespeare, by contrast, quickly gained a reputation in both
kinds. He also achieved fame with a unique innovation, the cycle
of dramas telling the story of the history of his own nation, mingling
nobles with commoners, moving from battles and usurpations
out of the history books to inventions of the tavern and the road,
such as the larger-than-life character of Sir John Falstaff and the
riotously comic incident of the highway robbery at Gadshill.

Shakespeare was widely admired in his own time, still more so
after the publication of the First Folio. But he was not initially
regarded as superior to all his contemporaries. Sir Richard Baker's
Chronicle of the Kings of England (1643) was representative
in judging that 'For writers of plays, and such as had been
players themselves, *William Shakespeare* and *Benjamin Jonson*,
have specially left their names recommended to posterity.'

Tragic inhibition, comic vitality

Shakespeare eventually eclipsed Jonson in both the library and the
theatre. The perceived greatness of his tragedies inhibited the
writing of new English tragedy for centuries. The dark, sexually
charged tragedies of his immediate successors have held the
stage – Thomas Middleton's *The Revenger's Tragedy* (1606–7),

Women Beware Women (1621), and *The Changeling* (1622, co-written with William Rowley); John Webster's *The White Devil* (1612) and *The Duchess of Malfi* (c. 1614); John Ford's *'Tis Pity She's a Whore* (1633) – but the closure of the theatres by the Puritans in 1642 prevented any further development for a generation. The neoclassical heroic tragedy that John Dryden and his contemporaries introduced to the English stage after the reopening of the theatres with the return of the monarchy in 1660 did not outlast its cultural moment. Milton's *Samson Agonistes* (1671) was a masterly conflation of biblical matter and Greek tragic form, but was never intended for the stage. Almost the only post-Restoration English tragedy to have held a place in the repertoire was Thomas Otway's skilfully neo-Shakespearean *Venice Preserved* (1682). The most honourable failures among the plethora of 18th- and 19th-century tragedies written under the shadow of Shakespeare were Percy Shelley's *The Cenci* (1819) and Lord Byron's historical dramas – but Byron's true dramatic métier lay with works such as *Manfred* (1817) and *Cain* (1821), written to be performed in the theatre of the imagination, not on the cavernous stages of Drury Lane and Covent Garden.

Henrik Ibsen's development of modern, bourgeois realist drama in the late 19th century inspired a new kind of tragedy in the Edwardian period, most notably in the work of the actor, theatre manager, director, and critic Harley Granville Barker (*The Voysey Inheritance*, 1905, about a financial scandal; and *Waste*, 1907, turning on a sex scandal that brings down a promising politician). Generally, though, the best-made plays in the repertoire of serious drama by English writers of the first half of the 20th century offered pathos rather than high tragedy – the cuckolded schoolmaster of Terence Rattigan's *The Browning Version* (1948), the constrained lovers in the railway station café in Noël Coward's *Still Life* (1936, filmed as *Brief Encounter*). The more ambitious innovations, such as T. S. Eliot's attempt to reinvent verse tragedy (*Murder in the Cathedral*, 1935), suffered from a certain dramatic clunkiness.

It took an Irishman to create a new kind of drama of genuinely Shakespearean philosophical reach, in which tragedy unfolds cheek by jowl with farce, and the language contrives to make austere beauty out of despair. In the sequence of plays that began with *Waiting for Godot* (1955) and *Endgame* (1957), Samuel Beckett's characters move across a precisely choreographed stage – or remain immobile upon it – in the manner of Lear and his Fool:

> **LEAR** Who is it that can tell me who I am?
> **FOOL** Lear's shadow.

Beckett, on 'the one theme' of his life: 'To and fro in shadow, from outer shadow to inner shadow. To and fro, between unattainable self and unattainable non-self.'

The history of post-Shakespearean English comedy is as rich as that of tragedy is sparse. It was shaped as much by Jonson's slick plotting and outrageous character types as by Shakespeare's disguises, self-discoveries, and witty sparring lovers – of whom Beatrice and Benedick in *Much Ado about Nothing* were the most influential. A succession of highly accomplished Restoration playwrights, including William Congreve, William Wycherley, Aphra Behn, and Susanna Centlivre, developed a distinct fusion of Jonsonian and Shakespearean comic techniques. The 18th-century theatre was animated by political satire (John Gay's *Beggar's Opera*, 1728), a mixture of sentimental lovers and lovable fools (such as Tony Lumpkin in Oliver Goldsmith's *She Stoops to Conquer*, 1773), and the dazzling wordplay of Richard Brinsley Sheridan (*The Rivals*, 1775, and *The School for Scandal*, 1777) and Hannah Cowley (*The Belle's Stratagem*, 1780). The comedy of manners was modernized by the irrepressible Irish wits Oscar Wilde (*The Importance of Being Earnest*, 1895) and George Bernard Shaw (*Pygmalion*, 1913). The line continues through Joe Orton's farces with a violent twist, Tom Stoppard's intellectual gymnastics, Michael Frayn's artful constructions, and beyond.

This story of failure in tragedy and success in comedy suggests that if there is such a thing as a national characteristic in English Literature, it is closely related to wit and humour. The transformation of comic stereotypes into rounded human beings (Sir Andrew Aguecheek's 'I was adored once too'); the magical theatrical coup ('One face, one voice, one habit, and two persons, / A natural perspective, that is and is not!' – *Twelfth Night* again); the ludicrous stage business (*'They faint alternately in one another's arms'* – Sheridan's *The Critic*); the one-liner and the witty aphorism delivered with impeccable timing ('A hand-bag?' ... 'To lose one parent, Mr Worthing, may be regarded as a misfortune; to lose both looks like carelessness' – Wilde's Lady Bracknell): nowhere is English Literature more sparklingly alive than in the comic theatre. This was certainly the view of William Hazlitt, who in 1818 delivered a pioneering set of *Lectures on the English Comic Writers*, in which he discerned the intimate connection between comic drama and a new literary form: the novel.

Chapter 8
Aspects of the English novel

Romance and novel

In December 1817, an advertisement appeared in the *Morning Chronicle* newspaper announcing the imminent publication of 'Northanger Abbey, a Romance; and Persuasion, a Novel. By the Author of Pride and Prejudice, Mansfield Park, etc.' Two things are striking about this: the anonymity of the author and the implied distinction between a novel and a romance. In Dr Johnson's *Dictionary of the English Language* half a century before, the novel was defined as 'a small tale, generally of love' and the romance as 'a tale of wild adventures in war and love'.

Johnson had a second definition for the word 'romance': 'a lie; a fiction'. Throughout his lifetime, there was a degree of arbitrariness as to whether prose fictions were called novels or romances, but many writers agreed that romances were more obviously lies or fictions. Romances involved 'miraculous Contingencies and impossible Performances', whereas 'Novels are of a more familiar nature; come near us, and represent to us Intrigues in practice, delight us with Accidents and odd Events, but not such as are wholly unusual or unprecedented' (William Congreve, preface to *Incognita: or, Love and Duty Reconciled. A Novel*, 1692). Romances revel in wild inventions, whilst novels purport to be true to real life. A book about terrifying adventures in a Gothic Abbey sounds as if it might be a romance; a book about a young lady being persuaded to make the correct choice of marital partner sounds much more like a novel. In fact, *Northanger Abbey* is the latter kind of book, not the former, and it was called neither a 'Novel' nor a 'Romance' on its title page. Jane Austen's author's note referred to it as a 'little work'.

For some commentators, both forms were 'trash'. Magazine columnists sounded off about 'Romances, Chocolate, Novels and the like Inflamers' (*The Spectator*, no. 365). Novels, like drinking chocolate, were a dangerously novel aphrodisiac – for females in particular. Women were indeed the majority consumers of 18th-century 'choc lit'. Thus Henry James Pye, a truly abysmal Poet Laureate, writing in 1792:

> the general effect of novel-reading on the gentler sex is too obvious to be doubted; it excites and enflames the passion which is the principal subject of the tale, and the susceptibility of the female votary of the circulating library, is proverbial.

In the light of such fulminations, it is understandable that a clergyman's daughter such as Jane Austen might prefer to keep her name off her title pages.

Romance was a very ancient literary form. If by a 'novel', we mean a prose narrative of some length, very often involving a love story and a plot that moves the characters between different locations, then the origins of the form may be traced back to the romances of the Hellenistic period. A typical example would be the adventures of Apollonius, told in many different versions, both classical and medieval. It was the ultimate source for William Shakespeare and George Wilkins' play *Pericles Prince of Tyre* (1608, also redacted as a prose narrative by Wilkins). Riddles and strangers, shipwrecks and mistaken identity, unlucky and lucky chances, quests and combats, danger and rescue, the whiff of incest, a movement between court intrigue and pastoral retreat,

SENSE

AND

SENSIBILITY:

A NOVEL.

IN THREE VOLUMES.

BY A LADY.

VOL. I.

London:

PRINTED FOR THE AUTHOR,

By C. Roworth, Bell-yard, Temple-bar,

AND PUBLISHED BY T. EGERTON, WHITEHALL.

1811.

7. Title page of Jane Austen's first published novel; her subsequent ones described her as the author of the previous ones, never naming her

the child lost and found, the resurrection of the apparently dead: this is the matter of romance. In Shakespeare's time, you could read dozens of stories of this kind in prose, often with interludes of poetry, then go to see them dramatized on stage. *The Winter's Tale* (1610) is based on Robert Greene's *Pandosto* (1588), but with a restorative 'Hollywood ending' that is Shakespeare's own.

A typical romance is peopled by dukes and princesses, often in disguise; the protagonist undergoes dramatic adventures in exotic settings. Magic and the supernatural often play a part. Since romances were escapist, unapologetically unrealistic, reading too many of them could give you a distorted view of what the world is really like. This thought was the starting point of Miguel de Cervantes' parody of the genre, *Don Quixote* (1605, English translation 1612). As an anti-romance, *Don Quixote* may be seen as a prototypical novel. Whereas the romance hero follows in the footsteps of Homer's Odysseus, travelling to mysterious Mediterranean islands and encountering otherworldly enchantresses, the novelistic hero follows in the footsteps of Don Quixote and his faithful companion Sancho Panza, travelling on ordinary roads and encountering down-to-earth innkeepers' wives. The road novel became a recognizable form of British literature in the 18th century, under the influence of the continental 'picaresque' tradition (a '*picaro*' was a roguish or lower-class hero). The Scotsman Tobias Smollett, who published translations of both *Don Quixote* and the archetypal French picaresque novel *Gil Blas*, was one of the pioneers, while the Englishman Henry Fielding was the master of the genre, with his naïve heroes Joseph Andrews and Tom Jones, and their respective companions, Parson Adams and Partridge.

The idea that character may be deformed by reading too many romances was domesticated and parodied in Charlotte Lennox's *The Female Quixote* (1752), the book that, according to the writer Anna Seward in an essay of 1787, 'gave the death's wound' to the 'declining taste' for the 'now totally exploded' genre of romance. Critics who report the death of a literary genre are usually rewarded by seeing it undergo a major revival within a few years. Anna Seward was no exception. The 1790s witnessed an explosion of romances. The queen of the form was Ann Radcliffe, author of *A Sicilian Romance* (1790), *The Romance of the Forest* (1791), *The Mysteries of Udolpho, a Romance* (1794), and *The Italian or the Confessional of the Black Penitents* (1796). These books later became known as 'Gothic novels', in allusion to Horace Walpole's pioneering *The Castle of Otranto: A Gothic Story* (1764), which located its horror story in a setting of medieval Gothic architecture (a style which Walpole revived in the design of his own house, Strawberry Hill).

A dark castle in a wild (and sublimely described) mountainous landscape. A young, innocent, beautiful, and brave heroine in isolation from her family and familiars. A brooding villain with a sinister secret in his past. Terrifying and seemingly supernatural events. These are the stock elements of Radcliffean romance. *But* the young lady's conduct is always impeccable, and you never really believe that she is going to be raped, as Clarissa was in Samuel Richardson's far less exotic but far more terrifying real tragic novel a generation before. The supernatural events in Mrs Radcliffe all turn out to have a rational explanation. That was how she rendered the form respectable – in sharp contrast to M. G. Lewis, whose *The Monk: A Romance* (1796) features a sex-maniac rapist monk, incest, demonic influence, the Wandering Jew, a castle of sadistic nuns, a rampaging mob, and the Spanish Inquisition. The Marquis de Sade, a connoisseur of the genre, considered *The Monk* to be the best book of its kind, not only on account of its juicy sex and violence, but also because of its implicit understanding that the bloody Terror of the French Revolution had rendered everyday reality so horrific that only the demonic and the supernatural were sufficient to create a greater horror in the realm of literature.

Northanger Abbey is a parody of the Gothic romance. There is no madwoman in the attic and the ancient chest contains not a

8. Female readers stimulated by Gothic: the copy of *The Monk* and the curling tongs on the table are equally calculated to make the hair stand on end (caricature by James Gillray)

hidden manuscript but a pile of crisply pressed laundry. Henry Tilney brings young Catherine Morland to her senses, and she realizes that

> Charming as were all Mrs Radcliffe's works, and charming even as were the works of all her imitators, it was not in them perhaps that human nature, at least in the Midland counties of England, was to be looked for. Of the Alps and Pyrenees, with their pine forests and their vices, they might give a faithful delineation; and Italy, Switzerland, and the south of France might be as fruitful in horrors as they were there represented. Catherine dared not doubt beyond her own country, and even of that, if hard pressed, would have yielded the northern and western extremities. But in the central part of England there was surely some security for the existence even of a wife not beloved, in the laws of the land, and the manners of the age. Murder was not tolerated, servants were not slaves, and neither

poison nor sleeping potions to be procured, like rhubarb, from every druggist.

No sooner has Catherine been disabused of her Gothic fantasies than, in a twist typical of Jane Austen's many-layered irony, she suffers the fate of a Gothic heroine: a tyrannical patriarch throws her out of the house in the middle of the night, without arranging transport home. General Tilney's motivation is not, however, that of a Gothic villain with a Satanic contract: he has merely discovered that Catherine does not have as much money as he has supposed, so will not bring the dowry he requires from a future daughter-in-law. Austen's realism about human nature trumps the world of romance. In *Sense and Sensibility*, she pulls a similar trick with regard to another modish fictional form of the time, the novel of extreme sensibility and Rousseauesque passion. Marianne Dashwood, the embodiment of sensibility, makes a marriage of sense to flannel-waistcoated Colonel Brandon. But at the same time, Elinor Dashwood, embodiment of sense, marries a mere clergyman for love as opposed to hitching herself to the master of a great house for money.

Charlotte Brontë disliked Austen's world because of its unromantic concern with marriage portions, annual income, decent behaviour, and strolling in manicured gardens as opposed to running wild on the moors. Mr Rochester is an extreme version of the kind of alluring but dangerous romantic hero (Willoughby, Wickham) whom Austen's heroines must learn to reject, though he is eventually tamed by fire and removed from the burnt shell of his Gothic pile to a peaceful domestic space in which Jane Eyre can be his ministering angel. Emily Brontë's *Wuthering Heights* (1847), by contrast, makes no such compromise. The genteel Lintons and their elegant house, Thrushcross Grange, are despised. The novel invests all its passion and energy in a psychologically intensified version of Gothic characters (brooding Heathcliff with his mysterious origins, Cathy ruled by heart rather than head), locations (the house on the moors, the landscape itself, the darkness, the grave), and apparatus (temporal setting a generation before the time of writing, narration within narration, ghosts, death in childbirth).

Together with its attack on romance, *Northanger Abbey* includes a defence of the novel:

> 'I am no novel-reader – I seldom look into novels – Do not imagine that I often read novels – It is really very well for a novel.' Such is the common cant. 'And what are you reading, Miss – ?' 'Oh! It is only a novel!' replies the young lady, while she lays down her book with affected indifference, or momentary shame. 'It is only *Cecilia*, or *Camilla*, or *Belinda*'; or, in short, only some work in which the greatest powers of the mind are displayed, in which the most thorough knowledge of human nature, the happiest delineation of its varieties, the liveliest effusions of wit and humour, are conveyed to the world in the best-chosen language.

The works cited here are novels by Frances (Fanny) Burney and Maria Edgeworth that deeply influenced Austen; her name appears in the list of subscribers printed at the front of Burney's *Camilla* (1796). Burney pioneered the novel of 'a young lady's entrance into the world' – the subtitle of her *Evelina* (1778). She taught Austen the art of writing from her heroine's point of view, but keeping the authorial voice at a distance from her. Austen perfected this in her wholly innovative use of a technique that has become known as 'free indirect discourse', whereby the narrative conveys the thoughts and feelings of the heroine with the immediacy that is usually found in first-person narration, but also passes ironic judgement on her by virtue of the third-person voice ('It darted through her, with the speed of an arrow, that Mr Knightley must marry no one but herself!' – *Emma*).

Burney was the first English novelist to write a self-conscious defence of the form itself. 'In the republic of letters', she began the preface to *Evelina*, there is no member of such inferior rank, or who is so much disdained by his brethren of the quill, as the humble Novelist; nor is his fate less hard in the world at large, since, among the whole class of writers, perhaps not one can be named of which the votaries are more numerous but less respectable.

Popularity in the marketplace equating with a lack of respect from the literary establishment: it is an enduring story. Burney effects a decisive break with tradition by appealing over the heads of arbiters of taste and potential patrons to 'the Public – for such, by novel writers, novel readers will be called'. She also dissociates the novel from the 'fantastic regions of Romance, where Fiction is coloured by all the gay tints of luxurious Imagination, where Reason is an outcast, and where the sublimity of the Marvellous rejects all aid from sober Probability'. And she defines the novelist's art: 'To draw characters from nature, though not from life, and to mark the manners of the times.' Realism, this is to say, but not the transposition into fiction of the facts of real people's lives in the style of what came to be called the *roman à clef* (novel with a key), a technique used to controversial effect by Delarivier Manley in her novels earlier in the century.

Paradoxically, despite the claim that the characters in *Evelina* were drawn from nature but not from life, Burney maintains the fiction that she is only the 'editor' of the collection of letters that constitute the narrative. This was a favoured device in epistolary fiction, used most elaborately by the genre's leading exponent Samuel Richardson, whose *Pamela* (1740, servant girl refuses to give in to sexual advances of her master and is eventually rewarded with marriage to him), *Clarissa* (1748, virtuous young woman abducted and raped by charismatic villain), and *Sir Charles Grandison* (1753–4, the story of a virtuous man) were the most influential English novels of the age. The 'editorial' device is intended to give the fiction an aura of verisimilitude. In Richardson's case, it breaks down the distinction between his novels and the collections of exemplary letters advising on manners and conduct that he had previously published. Analogously, Daniel Defoe had furnished *Robinson Crusoe* (1719) with maps in order to make it more like a true seaman's tale, just as his fiction of *Moll Flanders* (1722) was contrived to resemble the confessions of real-life criminals that were popular matter on early 18th-century bookstalls. In a sense, these were all devices for saying 'this book is real, it is not a fanciful romance'.

Henry Fielding had another way of evading the disreputable nomenclature 'novel' and 'romance': he called *Joseph Andrews* (1742) 'a comic epic in prose' and he furnished *Tom Jones* (1749) with comic versions of the apparatus of classical epic – invocations of the muse, a mighty battle, and so on. Prior to Burney, then, there was a reluctance to stand up and proclaim something to the effect of 'this book is a Novel, a new form of fiction that can portray human character and society with greater truth to the experience of the reading public than has ever been achieved before'.

The 'Condition of England'

In June 1829, the *Edinburgh Review* published an essay called 'Signs of the Times' by the Scotsman Thomas Carlyle. It argued, with unprecedented ferocity, that the 'mechanical age' – the Industrial Revolution – was destroying human individuality. England was in a state of moral crisis:

> The King has virtually abdicated; the Church is a widow, without jointure; public principle is gone; private honesty is going; society, in short, is in fact falling to pieces; and a time of unmixed evil is come on us.

In returning to this crisis in his later pamphlets *Chartism* (1840) and *Past and Present* (1843), Carlyle gave it a name: the 'Condition of England Question'. The mechanization of the human spirit, the high moral costs of industrial change: these were also the themes of some of the most powerful novels of the following decades, such as Elizabeth Gaskell's *Mary Barton* (1848) and *North and South* (1854), Charles Kingsley's *Alton Locke* (1854), Dickens' *Hard Times*, and George Eliot's *Felix Holt the Radical* (1866).

But the 19th-century novel more broadly is a Condition of England genre. The big house, sustained by the profits of a sugar plantation in the West Indies, in Jane Austen's *Mansfield Park* (1814) is England. The world in which Thomas Hardy's *Tess of the d'Urbervilles* (1891) is branded a fallen woman and his *Jude the Obscure* (1895) is excluded from university is England. The parsonage in which Mrs Humphrey Ward's *Robert Elsmere* (1888) loses his faith, in one of the bestsellers of the age, is England. Trollope's Barsetshire is an investigation into the condition of England, and so is Thackeray's *Vanity Fair* (1848), and so is H. G. Wells's futuristic *The Time Machine* (1895) with its class division between troglodyte Morlocks and effete leisured Eloi.

Bleak House (1853) is England: divided, as England has been for centuries, between country and city. Down in Chesney Wold, Lady Dedlock – an extreme version of the Lady Bertram of *Mansfield Park* – suffocates in the living death of boredom, harbouring a dark secret in her heart as the rain pours down the windows of the big house. John Ruskin would argue in a lecture called *The Storm-Cloud of the Nineteenth Century* (1884) that the carbon footprint of urbanization and industry has choked the moral life of the nation. The opening of *Bleak House* anticipates the thought, in Dickens' unique style. The fog is everywhere in London, both literally and metaphorically:

> London. Michaelmas term lately over, and the Lord Chancellor sitting in Lincoln's Inn Hall. Implacable November weather. As much mud in the streets as if the waters had but newly retired from the face of the earth, and it would not be wonderful to meet a

Megalosaurus, forty feet long or so, waddling like an elephantine lizard up Holborn Hill. Smoke lowering down from chimney-pots, making a soft black drizzle, with flakes of soot in it as big as full-grown snowflakes – gone into mourning, one might imagine, for the death of the sun....

Fog everywhere. Fog up the river, where it flows among green aits and meadows; fog down the river, where it rolls deified among the tiers of shipping and the waterside pollutions of a great (and dirty) city....

The raw afternoon is rawest, and the dense fog is densest, and the muddy streets are muddiest near that leaden-headed old obstruction, appropriate ornament for the threshold of a leaden-headed old corporation, Temple Bar. And hard by Temple Bar, in Lincoln's Inn Hall, at the very heart of the fog, sits the Lord High Chancellor in his High Court of Chancery.

But out of the darkness, Dickens conjures life, an array of characters more eclectic and bizarre than literature had ever seen before. Krook, who spontaneously combusts. Guppy, eager like a puppy. Mrs Jellyby, the 'telescopic philanthropist' whose project to educate the natives of Borrioboola-Gha causes her to neglect her own family. Jo the homeless crossing sweeper, lowest of the low in the social order, but harbouring the key to the secret of the true identity of Nemo, the man with no name, a secret that will unlock the closed heart of Lady Dedlock, rouse her from torpor, and take her to love and death in a cold and bitter London graveyard. Tulkinghorn, the devious lawyer. Inspector Bucket: a type who would become very familiar in later English fiction, the detective. And dozens more. As the novelist George Gissing said, everything Dickens looked upon 'was registered in his mind'.

In the summer of 1845, Dickens triumphed onstage in the role of the braggart Captain Bobadil in an amateur production – cast, produced, and directed by himself – of Ben Jonson's *Every Man in His Humour*. Dickens loved the theatre more than anything, as may be guessed from his affectionate portrayal of theatre folk in *Nicholas Nickleby* (1839). His comic types, often with names that reveal their personalities, are inherited from Jonson's comedy of humours. The English novel has theatre in its bones: Fielding became a novelist because his theatrical career was cut short by the 1737 Licensing Act; Richardson's Lovelace models himself on the rakes of the Restoration stage; Burney would rather have been a playwright than a novelist; Jane Austen avidly attended the theatre, constructed her novels in the form of scenes, and read her dialogue aloud with family and friends. But Dickens was the most theatrical of them all, eventually turning the highlights of his novels into a one-man show at packed public readings.

Writing about one of Dickens' most memorable grotesques, Mrs Gamp in *Our Mutual Friend* (1865), Gissing argued that humour is inseparable from charity. Humour not only enabled Dickens 'to see this coarse creature as an amusing person', it also, more

9. The novel as drama: Dickens at a public reading

profoundly, 'inspired him with that large tolerance which looks through things external, gives its full weight to circumstance, and preserves a modesty, a humility, in human judgment'. This may not be true as a generalization about humour. The savage indignation of Jonathan Swift, or of Martin Amis in *Money* (1984), is not exactly characterized by large tolerance and humility in judgement. But it is true of many of the great English comic novels – let us say, George and Weedon Grossmith's *Diary of a Nobody* (1892), Evelyn Waugh's *Decline and Fall* (1928), Stella Gibbons' *Cold Comfort Farm* (1932), P. G. Wodehouse's *The Code of the Woosters* (1938), Nancy Mitford's *The Pursuit of Love* (1945). And it is true in spades of Dickens.

The novels of Dickens are protests against child labour, social inequality, poverty, malice, dirt, and English hypocrisy. But they have a soft-centred heart and usually end in the distribution of rewards (surprise legacies for the deserving). There is another side to the art of the novel, in which the profoundest understanding of the complexity of individuals, their relationships and their social milieu, requires a commitment to human intelligence.

Middlemarch: A Study of Provincial Life (1872) sounds from its title as if it will be a Condition of Middle England novel, but it turns out to be much more than that. The story of Dorothea Brooke domesticates classical tragedy. As George Eliot explains in the novel's prelude, Dorothea is a latter-day St Theresa, living 'a life of mistakes, the offspring of a certain spiritual grandeur ill-matched with the meanness of opportunity': 'helped by no coherent social faith and order which could perform the function of knowledge for the ardently willing soul', she alternates 'between a vague ideal and the common yearning of womanhood; so that the one was disapproved as extravagance, and the other condemned as a lapse'. When the Condition of England is such that there is 'no coherent social faith and order', the novelist must step in and create an order, a manageable world. The novel can provide a 'certain spiritual grandeur' that is unthreatened by the proposition that we might be descended from apes rather than fashioned by the hand of God. The man whom George Eliot married late in life gives us some sense of the work that such a creation required:

> She told me that, in all that she considered her best writing, there was a 'not herself' which took possession of her, and that she felt her own personality to be merely the instrument through which this spirit, as it were, was acting. Particularly she dwelt on this in regard to the scene in *Middlemarch* between Dorothea and Rosamond, saying that, although she always knew they had, sooner or later, to come together, she kept the idea resolutely out of her mind until Dorothea was in Rosamond's drawing-room. Then, abandoning herself to the inspiration of the moment, she wrote the whole scene exactly as it stands, without alteration or erasure, in an intense state of excitement and agitation, feeling herself entirely possessed by the feelings of the two women.... With this sense of 'possession', it is easy to imagine what the cost to the author must have been of writing books, each of which has its tragedy.
>
> (J. W. Cross, *George Eliot's Life as related in her Letters and Journals*, 1884)

This is what the very greatest literature can do: a force that is somehow 'not herself' takes 'possession' of the writer and enables her to create a second world that has the power to take 'possession' of the reader in turn, and to transport us out of our own world in such a way that when we return home, we sense that we have become more human, more emotionally intelligent. Guided by the living hand of George Eliot, the novel is a place where the dedicated reader finds a new, if provisional, coherence.

The stream of consciousness

'On or about December 1910 human nature changed', wrote Virginia Woolf in her essay 'Mr Bennett and Mrs Brown' (1924). 'All human relations shifted, and when human relations change there is at the same time a change in religion, conduct, politics, and literature.' Arnold Bennett's realistic Edwardian novels of provincial life contained too much clutter. The furniture gets in the way of the creation of the inner life. So Woolf argues: to create 'a flesh-and-blood Mrs Brown', you have to abandon the externals and embrace the full complexity and incoherence of the inner life – about which Sigmund Freud was teaching the Modern age.

Woolf's imagined character Mrs Brown is in some sense a response to James Joyce's Mr and Mrs Bloom in *Ulysses*, though Woolf harboured some upper-middle-class reservations about the Irishman's broad language and his harping on bodily functions. There was just a little too much flesh-and-blood in Joyce for Woolf's genteel taste. But in an essay on 'Modern Fiction', written after the publication of *Dubliners* and before that of *Ulysses*, she praised him for his ability to dwell in the moment: 'let us record the atoms as they fall on the mind in the order in which they fall, let us trace the pattern, however disconnected and incoherent in appearance, which each sight or incident scores upon the consciousness'. Woolf's belief that it was the modern writer's task to catch the 'moment of being' accounts for her witty conceit of locating the onset of modernity in a particular moment, around the time of the death of stuffy old King Edward VII.

In his Edwardian novels, Henry James, an American in Sussex, had perfected Jane Austen's art of being simultaneously inside and outside a character through the technique of rendering first-person thoughts in a third-person voice, so as to achieve a previously impossible union of sympathetic identification and ironic detachment. A key sentence in James's essay 'The Art of Fiction' (1884) took the interior life towards its Modernist form:

> Experience is never limited and it is never complete; it is an immense sensibility, a kind of huge spider-web of the finest silken threads suspended in the chamber of consciousness, catching every air-borne particle in its tissue.

This is a clear anticipation of Virginia Woolf's manifesto for the stream-of-consciousness novel, of which *Ulysses* is the towering example.

In 1983, the philosopher of mind Daniel Dennett delivered a paper at a symposium on consciousness in which he argued that the human self is nothing more or less than the 'centre of narrative gravity' within the brain. In a profound sense, everyone is a novelist: 'Our tales are spun, but for the most part we don't spin them; they spin us', wrote Dennett when further developing the idea in his book *Consciousness Explained* (1991), 'Our human consciousness, and our narrative selfhood, is their product, not their source.' He called this a 'multiple drafts' theory of consciousness, which sounds a very literary idea.

Another investigator of consciousness, the neurophysiologist Antonio Damasio, has argued in his books *Descartes's Error* (1994) and *The Feeling of What Happens* (2001) that the division between reason and passion, cognition and emotion – an opposition that goes all the way back to Aristotle – is, from a neurological point of view, a fallacy. Damasio and his colleagues have shown that emotion is integral to the processes of reasoning and decision-making, for worse and for better. René Descartes' Enlightenment fantasy of a disembodied mind is equally fallacious: the mind only makes consciousness through the body, which is the theatre of our emotions – as manifested most obviously by a blush, or for that matter an erection (two phenomena which fascinated John Keats and James Joyce). Furthermore, cognitive activity is structured by image schemata that are themselves structured by bodily experience. The brain is not like a computer because a computer does not have a body. These are things that may be inferred not only from the empirical research of early 21st-century brain scientists, but also from the work of early 20th-century novelists.

'The self in our stream of consciousness changes continuously as it moves forward in time, even as we retain a sense that the self remains the same while our existence continues': this is Damasio's paraphrase of William James's observation about one of the paradoxes of consciousness. Damasio proposes a resolution to this paradox by means of a division between the 'core self' and a higher-level 'autobiographical self', for which a neuroanatomical basis may be inferred from cases when brain damage has wiped out 'autobiographical' knowledge but left core functioning intact. It was William James who coined the phrase 'stream of consciousness': in certain respects, he anticipated Damasio's account of the interdependence of brain, body, and emotion, just as his brother Henry James brought unprecedented rigour to the question of how the novelist can represent consciousness.

The image of the stream moving through time raises a key question for the self-conscious novelist: how do you represent time in narrative? Joyce proposed one answer by setting the entire mock epic narrative of *Ulysses* on a single day:

> In using the myth, in manipulating a continuous parallel between contemporaneity and antiquity, Mr Joyce is pursuing a method which others must pursue after him... It is simply a way of controlling, of ordering, of giving a shape and a significance to the immense panorama of futility and anarchy which is contemporary history.

(T. S. Eliot, 'Ulysses, Order, and Myth', 1923)

Virginia Woolf tried another in *Orlando: A Biography* (1928), a fantasia about her friend and lover Vita Sackville-West, which is at once an anticipation of late 20th-century fictional 'magic realism' and a playful 'Very Short Introduction to English Literature'.

Orlando is an Elizabethan nobleman, with a little bit of peasant 'Kentish or Sussex earth' in his genetic mix. He is acquainted with Shakespeare and dabbles in the writing of tragedies confounded with horrid plots and suffused with noble sentiments.

In the 17th century, he immerses himself in the 'marvellously contorted cogitations of Sir Thomas Browne'. After the Restoration, which is to say in the era when Aphra Behn became (according to Woolf) the first professional woman writer, Orlando turns into a woman. In the 18th century, he moves in high society but is bored by the vacuous wit of his peers. In the 19th century, the weather changes. Damp takes hold everywhere:

> Stealthily and imperceptibly...the constitution of England was altered and nobody knew it. Everywhere the effects were felt. The hardy country gentleman, who had sat down gladly to a meal of ale and beef in a room designed, perhaps by the brothers Adam, with classic dignity, now felt chilly. Rugs appeared; beards were grown; trousers were fastened tight under the instep. The chill which he felt in his legs the country gentleman soon transferred to his house; furniture was muffled; walls and tables were covered; nothing was left bare.... Coffee supplanted the after-dinner port, and, as coffee led to a drawing-room in which to drink it, and a drawing-room to glass cases, and glass cases to artificial flowers, and artificial flowers to mantelpieces, and mantelpieces to pianofortes, and pianofortes to drawing-room ballads, and drawing-room ballads (skipping a stage or two) to innumerable little dogs, mats, and china ornaments, the home – which had become extremely important – was completely altered.

> Outside the house – it was another effect of the damp – ivy grew in unparalleled profusion. Houses that had been of bare stone were smothered in greenery.... The damp struck within. Men felt the chill in their hearts; the damp in their minds.... Love, birth, and death were all swaddled in a variety of fine phrases. The sexes drew further and further apart. No open conversation was tolerated. Evasions and concealments were sedulously practised on both sides.... Thus the British Empire came into existence; and thus – for there is no stopping damp; it gets into the inkpot as it gets into the woodwork – sentences swelled, adjectives multiplied, lyrics became epics, and little trifles that had been essays a column long were now encyclopaedias in ten or twenty volumes.

Orlando survives even the chilly Victorian age. The book ends with her in the present, in the moment. A clock strikes and she catches at the impressions that constitute consciousness:

> She saw two flies circling round and noticed the blue sheen on their bodies; she saw a knot in the wood where her foot was, and her dog's ear twitching. At the same time, she heard a bough creaking in the garden, a sheep coughing in the park, a swift screaming past the window.... She noticed the separate grains of earth in the flower beds as if she had a microscope stuck to her eye.... Braced and strung up by the present moment she was also strangely afraid, as if whenever the gulf of time gaped and let a second through some unknown danger might come with it. The tension was too relentless and too rigorous to be endured long without discomfort. She walked more briskly than she liked, as if her legs were moved for her, through the garden and out into the park.

She has become a character in a Virginia Woolf novel.

The close relationship between fiction and 'true life' travel narratives and criminal lives in the 18th century reminded Woolf of the kinship between novel and biography, or 'life-writing', as she preferred to call it. From *Tom Jones* to *David Copperfield*, to D. H. Lawrence's *Sons and Lovers* (1913), to Joyce's *Portrait of the Artist as a Young Man* (1916), novels have often followed the protagonist's growth to maturity in the manner of a biography. Many a novel has been called 'the life of' or 'the history of' such and such a character, who has sometimes been a projection of the author him- or herself. Orlando's immortality and gender-bending parody the cradle-to-grave structure that can deaden both novel and biography; Woolf is shaking up received novelistic practice rather as her friend Lytton Strachey shook up life-writing in his *Eminent Victorians* (1918). She happily imagines a hero(ine) who lives for centuries because she knows that there has been something absurd about the attempt at verisimilitude in the representation of time in the novel ever since Richardson's Pamela and Clarissa gave the impression of spending more time writing about their experiences than experiencing them.

From its outset, the English novel has been as interested in the unreliability as the authenticity of narratorial voice. Is Pamela really as virtuous as she makes out, or might she be using her sexuality in order to lure Mr B. into marriage, thus achieving social advancement and financial security for herself and her family? That was Henry Fielding's reading of Richardson in his parody *Shamela* (1741). More subtly and insinuatingly, how far can we trust the narrative consciousness of Briony Tallis in Ian McEwan's *Atonement* (2001)?

The preface to *Orlando* begins with an acknowledgement of obligations of the kind one often finds in biographies, but with a twist:

> Many friends have helped me in writing this book. Some are dead and so illustrious that I scarcely dare name them, yet no one can read or write without being perpetually in the debt of Defoe, Sir Thomas Browne, Sterne, Sir Walter Scott, Lord Macaulay, Emily Brontë, De Quincey, and Walter Pater, – to name the first that come to mind.

On the matter of time, consciousness, and the novel, the most revealing of these names is that of Sterne.

Consider the problem of autobiography. Every second I spend writing my autobiography adds a second to my life, so how can my narrative ever catch up with me and allow me to complete my story? The complete biography, autobiography, or novel would catch every impression that has written itself on the mind of the subject and associated itself with other impressions in order to create their story, their self. But no narrative could ever catch more than the tiniest proportion of this material. And when should the story of a life begin? At birth? Or conception? Or should one try to explain the background to the moment of conception. Let us say that a man is in the habit of performing two actions every Sunday night, the first being to wind up a clock, the second being to make love to his wife. Let us then suppose that one night he realizes in the middle of performing the second action that he has forgotten to execute the first, and that the business is therefore somewhat unfinished, though finished enough to have conceived a child, who, influenced by the moment of conception, will habitually fail to finish anything at all, let alone the writing of his own complete life story.

Laurence Sterne's *The Life and Opinions of Tristram Shandy, Gentleman* (1759–67) is a parody of the novel before the novel was fully born. It is both a condition of humanity novel and a stream-of-consciousness novel. And it is a book that is acutely self-conscious about the possibilities and limitations of the book as

10. The black page marking Yorick's death in *Tristram Shandy*

a medium of communication. Everyone has their own idea of beauty, so if you want a description of a beautiful woman, why not leave a blank page and allow each reader to fill it in with a description of their own? If a loved character dies, we should stop to mourn them, so why not allow the book itself to wear mourning black for a moment?

'Nothing odd will do long', said Dr Johnson, '*Tristram Shandy* did not last'. On this occasion, he was wrong: the very singularity of *Tristram Shandy* has made it a renewable resource, a font of the incomparable diversity of the English novel.

Chapter 9
The Englishness of English Literature?

'England, my England?'

> What have I done for you,
> England, my England?
> What is there I would not do,
> England, my own?

('Pro rege nostro', 1892)

So wrote the tubercular imperialist William Ernest Henley, author of 'Invictus' ('I am the master of my fate: / I am the captain of my soul'). But whose England is that of English Literature?

For centuries, the most widely read work in the repertoire was *Pilgrim's Progress* by John Bunyan, son of a tinker, barely schooled, dissenter from the Anglican articles of faith, itinerant preacher imprisoned for his activities, decried as a witch and a highwayman. The most commercially successful poet of the 18th century was Alexander Pope, a four-foot-six-inch Roman Catholic hunchback. The most famous poet of the 19th century was Lord Byron, a Scottish Calvinist exile from the English high society that he scorned, that bitched about him, but that could not get enough of his charisma.

England, my England: in 1922, the miner's son and apostle of sexual freedom D. H. Lawrence allusively but ironically gave the title to a collection of his short stories. Lawrence was, as he wrote to Lady Cynthia Asquith that same year, 'English in the teeth of all the world, even in the teeth of England'. He loathed English gentility, English class prejudice, English repression of sex, English prudery about the language of sex. Yet he loved the English land. The protagonist of the collection's title story hates war but still enlists and dies in Flanders. 'He had no conception of Imperial England, and Rule Britannia was just a joke to him', and yet he has an instinctive faith in 'the lost, intense sensations of the primeval people of the place, whose passions seethed in the air still, from those long days before the Romans came. The seethe of a lost, dark passion in the air. The presence of unseen snakes.'

'England your England': the title of the first part of Old Etonian George Orwell's *The Lion and the Unicorn: Socialism and the English Genius*, written during the Blitz in 1940. 'The diversity of it, the chaos!' Orwell's five fragments of 'the English scene' are a Lancashire mill town, trucks on the Great North Road, queues outside the job centre, pinball machines in a Soho pub, and 'old maids biking to Holy Communion through the mists of the autumn morning'. England: you hate it, you laugh at it, says Orwell, his emotions concentrated by the war, but you belong to it and will never get away from it until you die.

English Literature: the home not only of nostalgia, belonging, and sceptical accommodation, but also of dissent, ridicule, self-hatred, rebellion, and alienation.

Since the Second World War, the 'English scene', as Orwell calls it, has been rich in loathing and laughter. The most influential novels of the 1950s – Kingsley Amis's *Lucky Jim* (1954), Alan Sillitoe's *Saturday Night and Sunday Morning* (1958) – simmer with rage, fuelled by drink and low expectations. As for the

Englishman abroad, he is compromised and broken: Malcolm Lowry's alcoholic ex-consul in Mexico (*Under the Volcano*, 1947), Graham Greene's embittered journalist in Vietnam (*The Quiet American*, 1955).

England, whose England? In the half-century following the end of empire, a new chorus of voices was heard: immigrants to Britain, former colonial subjects in newly independent states, the children of immigrants – from Samuel Selvon (*The Lonely Londoners*, 1956) and Chinua Achebe (*Things Fall Apart*, 1958), to Zadie Smith (*White Teeth*, 2000) and Andrea Levy (*Small Island*, 2004). 'Inglan is a bitch / Dere's no escapin' it': the immigrant Caribbean performance poet Linton Kwesi Johnson damns English racism even as he makes his home in the nation of dog lovers and bulldog breeders.

In *Parade's End* (1924–8), Ford Madox Ford's magnificent novel sequence anatomizing the last of England, the quintessential Englishman (with a Dutch name) Christopher Tietjens describes the village of Bemerton in Wiltshire, where George Herbert was a country parson, as 'the cradle of the race as far as our race was worth thinking about'. Bemerton is now a suburb of Salisbury rather than a self-contained village. The Orwellian old maid biking to Holy Communion through the mists of the autumn morning is at risk of being knocked over by the car of the hurrying commuter. And what of the rectory? The Church of England has sold off its finest rural properties. In 1996, George Herbert's residence was bought and renovated by the cosmopolitan polyglot Indian-born Hindu-bred bisexual poet and novelist Vikram Seth. He paid for it with the proceeds of *A Suitable Boy* (1993), a novel that stands – not least in length – beside Samuel Richardson's *Clarissa* as a monument to the art of English fiction.

Literature, the cradle of the culture if not the race, has been repossessed and renovated by midnight's children.

Literature in English?

In 1955, the German-Jewish refugee Nikolaus Pevsner delivered a series of Reith Lectures on BBC radio entitled 'The Englishness of English Art'. He sought to anatomize the national character by ways of its art and architecture, grounding his observations in climate and landscape. But he encountered such variety that he reached few conclusions about Englishness beyond 'love of nature', exemplified by John Constable, and a gift for the grotesque, exemplified by William Hogarth. A series of lectures on the Englishness of English Literature would face even more variety and probably manage little more in the way of a conclusion than some analogous remarks about the distinctive sense of place in English poetry and the pervasive sense of humour in English prose.

But it would probably founder even before it began, not least because of the problem of defining what is meant by *English* literature.

Does it mean literature written in the English language? Herman Melville's *Moby Dick*, Henry David Thoreau's *Walden, or Life in the Woods*, Emily Dickinson's poetry, F. Scott Fitzgerald's *The Great Gatsby*, Arthur Miller's *Death of a Salesman*. By any account, they are literature, and English is the language that they use with wonderful resourcefulness. But they have to be classified as American Literature, not English.

Henry James and T. S. Eliot were born in America, but moved to England and won high honours as British citizens. When do they become part of English Literature? When they start writing in England, or writing about England? When they are published in England, or when they take on citizenship? And what about Sylvia Plath? She was a deeply American writer, but her best poems were written in her last days in Devon and London and were deeply bound up with her marriage to a British poet, which entitled her to travel under his passport.

Or does it mean literature written by English people?

There is a large body of literature written by English people over several centuries in languages other than English, most notably Latin. Are we to say that Sir Thomas More's *Utopia* was not part of English Literature when written in Latin in 1513, but became part of it when Ralph Robinson translated the text into English in 1551? That Andrew Marvell's 'The Garden' is a work of English Literature, but that 'Hortus', his own Latin version of the same poem, is not?

Who were the first English-born poets to have their works published in a complete edition, in the manner of the classics of Greece and Rome? The usual answer to this question is either Samuel Daniel (*Workes*, 1601) or Ben Jonson (*Workes*, 1616). But what about Elizabeth Jane Weston (1581–1612)? Her collected poems, published in 1602, were admired across Europe. Is *Poëmata Elisabethae Joannae Westoniae Anglae, virginis nobilissimae, poëtriae celeberrimae, linguarum plurimarum peritissimae, studio ac opera* ('Poems of Elizabeth Jane Weston, Englishwoman, most noble virgin, most celebrated poet, most skilled in many languages, studies and works', 1602) habitually left out of the story of English Literature because Weston wrote in Latin or because she spent most of her working life abroad, at the court of Rudolph II in Prague? Or for both reasons?

English Nobels?

Consider the apparently unexceptionable proposition 'what we mean by *English* Literature may be exemplified by listing the citizens of these islands who have won the Nobel Prize for Literature'. Here they are, in chronological order of award.

Rudyard Kipling was awarded the prize in 1907 'in consideration of the power of observation, originality of imagination, virility of ideas and remarkable talent for narration which characterizes the creations of this world-famous author'. Born in Bombay (Mumbai), Kipling began his autobiography by addressing Allah. The community in which he felt most at home was the Freemasons because his 'brethren' there were 'Muslims, Hindus, Sikhs, members of the Araya and Brahmo Samaj, and a Jew' (*Something of Myself*). Even in his most imperial work, his contribution to Fletcher's *History of England*, he identified himself not with the English establishment but with a Roman centurion on the distant edge of empire. When called back to Rome, the centurion realizes that 'time, custom, grief and toil, age, memory, service, love, / Have rooted me in British soil'. By the same account, in his emotions Kipling was always called back to India, where he was born and where he first worked. He described his boarding school in England as 'the House of Desolation'. When he returned to Bombay at the age of sixteen, the sights and smells of home 'made me deliver in the vernacular sentences whose meaning I knew not'. He was rooted in Indian soil.

Next came William Butler Yeats (1923) 'for his always inspired poetry, which in a highly artistic form gives expression to the spirit of a whole nation'. Yeats was an Irishman, who served in the Senate of the Irish Free State. Admittedly, he came from the Protestant Anglo-Irish ascendancy, with the result that many republicans and nationalists would challenge the claim that he gave expression to the spirit of the whole nation, especially as he did not write in Gaelic. Whatever the merits of that argument, the nation in question was Ireland, not England or Great Britain or the United Kingdom.

George Bernard Shaw (1925) 'for his work which is marked by both idealism and humanity, its stimulating satire often being infused with a singular poetic beauty'. Another Irishman.

John Galsworthy (1932) 'for his distinguished art of narration which takes its highest form in *The Forsyte Saga*'. Born in Surrey to a prosperous middle-class family. Harrow School and Oxford University. The first trueborn Englishman to win the prize.

Thomas Stearns Eliot (1948) 'for his outstanding, pioneering contribution to present-day poetry'. Born in St Louis, Missouri.

Bertrand Russell (1950) 'in recognition of his varied and significant writings in which he champions humanitarian ideals and freedom of thought'. His achievement was philosophical and to some degree political, not literary, so we may set him aside.

Winston Churchill (1953) 'for his mastery of historical and biographical description as well as for brilliant oratory in defending exalted human values'. Here we may set aside the question of the literary merits of Churchill's historical and biographical works: the point is that he was half-American. His mother was the daughter of a New York financier whose ancestors had fought against the British in the American War of Independence. According to an unproven family tradition that was believed by Churchill himself, his grandmother was of Iroquois descent.

Samuel Beckett (1969) 'for his writing, which – in new forms for the novel and drama – in the destitution of modern man acquires its elevation'. Beckett was an Irishman who lived most of his life in France, and wrote many of his works in French before translating them into English.

Elias Canetti (1981) 'for writings marked by a broad outlook, a wealth of ideas and artistic power'. Canetti was a Bulgarian-born Sephardi Jew whose mother tongue was Ladino and who wrote in German, but he came to London to escape the Nazis and took British citizenship in 1952 – though he spent the last twenty years of his life in Zurich.

William Golding (1983) 'for his novels which, with the perspicuity of realistic narrative art and the diversity and universality of myth, illuminate the human condition in the world of today'. Born in Cornwall, which was once an independent principality, but went to grammar school and Oxford, so qualifies as only the second genuinely English winner of the prize.

Seamus Heaney (1995) 'for works of lyrical beauty and ethical depth, which exalt everyday miracles and the living past'. Heaney was born in Ulster – as a Roman Catholic. He moved to the Republic of Ireland and declined to be included in a *Penguin Book of Contemporary British Poetry* (1982), writing a light-toned but seriously intended poem that explained why:

> be advised,
> My passport's green
> No glass of ours was ever raised
> To toast the Queen ...
> You'll understand I draw the line
> At being robbed of what is mine,
> My patria ...
>
> (*An Open Letter*, 1983)

He let it be known that he would decline the office of Poet Laureate, which Prime Minister Tony Blair wished to offer him after the death of Ted Hughes.

V. S. Naipaul (2001) 'for having united perceptive narrative and incorruptible scrutiny in works that compel us to see the presence of suppressed histories'. A longtime resident of Wiltshire, but born in Trinidad into a family who, just two generations earlier, had been transported from India to the West Indies as indentured labourers. Naipaul's finest work is written from the point of view of the outsider – of his father as a Trinidadian of Indian extraction (*A House for Mr Biswas*, 1961), of himself as an immigrant in Britain (*The Enigma of Arrival*, 1987), and, controversially, as a visitor to India (the trilogy *An Area of Darkness*, *India: A Wounded Civilization*, and *India: A Million Mutinies Now*, 1964–90).

Harold Pinter (2005) 'who in his plays uncovers the precipice under everyday prattle and forces entry into oppression's closed rooms'. Though authentically English by virtue of being born in Hackney in the East End of London, his grandparents were Ashkenazic Jews from Poland and Odessa. His mother was born with the surname Moskowitz, and he published his early poems under the names Pinta and da Pinto.

Doris Lessing (2007) 'that epicist of the female experience, who with skepticism, fire and visionary power has subjected a divided civilization to scrutiny'. Lessing was born in Persia (now Iran) and brought up in Southern Rhodesia (now Zimbabwe). The surname under which she writes is that of her second husband, who later became East German ambassador to Uganda, where he was murdered during the uprising against Idi Amin. A divided civilization indeed.

In short, no English-born poet has ever won the Nobel Prize for Literature, except Pinter, who was honoured for his plays, not his technically weaker and more crudely political poems. The only unequivocally English novelists to have done so are Galsworthy and Golding. From the vantage point of posterity, it is astonishing that the essentially Edwardian figure of Galsworthy should have been honoured in 1932, by which time D. H. Lawrence, Dorothy Richardson, James Joyce, Ford Madox Ford, Virginia Woolf, and others had transformed the English novel. Posterity is also highly likely to judge that the English novelist who did most to 'illuminate the human condition' in the second half of the 20th century was not William Golding but J. G. Ballard, who anatomized England so incisively in part because he was always an outsider, having spent his childhood in China, including several years in an internment camp. Of course, these choices say something about the oddity of prizes that are awarded by committees – and, in the early years of the award especially, there was the added distortion of the stipulation in Alfred Nobel's will that the prize should be awarded for literature 'of an idealistic tendency' – but the serendipitous ethnic and geographical variety of the list says much about the cultural diversity that is embodied under the rubric English Literature. Performing the exercise on the Nobel laureates of any other nation would uncover a far greater degree of homogeneity.

British Literature?

The Nobel Prize has symbolic value as a mark of international acclaim. Had there been such an award in the 19th century, the leading English-language contender for it would have been a Scotsman: Sir Walter Scott, the most widely read and influential historical novelist of the age. The Scottishness of Scott and of Robert Burns, the Irishness of Yeats and Shaw and Oscar Wilde and James Joyce, the Welshness of Dylan Thomas and R. S. Thomas, has led some to propose the category of 'British Literature' as opposed to English. In university departments in the United States, one sometimes finds the distinction between courses in American Literature and those in British Literature.

This attempt at Celtophile inclusiveness is unhelpful because it is unhistorical, as may be seen simply by asking whether William Shakespeare thought of himself as an English or a British playwright. The answer to this question is that during the reign of Queen Elizabeth I, he considered himself English, and indeed devoted a large portion of his writing time to plays that dramatized the history of England, but that in the early years of the reign of James VI of Scotland as James I of England, Shakespeare began writing about 'British' matter (notably in *King Lear* and *Cymbeline*) because James had hopes of creating a British state. Those hopes were dashed by the parliaments in both London and Edinburgh. The British state did not come into being until 1707 (except, briefly and somewhat theoretically, in republican form between 1654 and 1660), so it is anachronistic to speak of 'British Literature' from before the 18th century.

Storytelling has always played an important part in the shaping of national identity. The Victorians believed in a seamless bond between 'our English Literature' and 'our island story'. But, as modern historians have frequently emphasized, the forms of nationhood within these islands have been highly varied. Every different state formation – English, Welsh, Scottish, Irish, British, 'United Kingdom', Tudor, Stuart, republican, constitutional, monarchical, parliamentary – has had its own narratives of identity and belonging.

For several centuries, the English/British were part of a theological entity called 'Christendom', which was often assumed (incorrectly) to overlap with a geographical entity called 'Europe'. English members of the original diasporic nation, the Jews, have long been considered 'outsiders' because they do not belong to 'Christendom': this is a key point in several major 19th-century novels, most notably *Daniel Deronda* (1876) by George Eliot, *Reuben Sachs* (1889) by Amy Levy (a Jew, writing in conscious reaction against Eliot), and *The Wondrous Tale of Alroy* (1833), *Coningsby* (1844), and *Tancred* (1847) by Benjamin Disraeli (a Jew by birth though baptized a Christian in his teens).

Given the potential for confusion and offence in the islands' many political dispensations over the centuries, some scholars have proposed abandoning the terms 'English Literature' and 'British Literature' altogether, speaking instead of something like 'the Literature of the north-east Atlantic archipelago'. That is probably too much of a mouthful to catch on; nevertheless, before describing any work as a contribution to 'English Literature', it might be worth asking under which national formation it was created.

Geoffrey Chaucer wrote *The Canterbury Tales* between 1386 and 1400 while he was a servant at the court of King Richard II, where the predominant language of the interlinked arts of courtiership and poetry was French.

Andrew Marvell wrote what has been considered the best political poem in the English language, in addition to the most memorable of all Renaissance English poems on the theme of *carpe diem* ('seize the day'), and a series of profound meditations on the relationship between the human mind and the natural world. These poems – 'An Horatian Ode upon Cromwell's Return from Ireland', 'To his Coy Mistress', 'The Garden', the 'Mower' poems, and 'Upon Appleton House' – may all have been composed in the space of just over a year (summer 1650 to summer 1651), when Marvell was living in his native Yorkshire at the time of greatest political uncertainty in English history: between the execution of King Charles I and the establishment of Oliver Cromwell as Lord Protector. Marvell's small body of highly wrought work constitutes English poetry's most concentrated imaginative investigation of the conflicting demands of the active and the contemplative life, the self and society, the force of desire and the pressure of mortality, the detached mind and the body embedded in its environment. They are poems that belong to all time, but that are also deeply marked by their own particular historical moment ('The Garden' less than the others, and it is the one poem in the group that may have been written later, possibly indeed after the Restoration of the monarchy in 1660).

Around the same time, Katherine Philips, who was born in London but lived deep in rural Wales, wrote royalist poetry whilst her husband was serving as an active, if moderate, Parliamentarian. John Milton, meanwhile, was a dedicated servant of Oliver Cromwell. After the Restoration, he wrote *Paradise Lost* (1667): a poem about all time, from the primal war in Heaven to the Last Judgement, a poem that has endured through centuries, but again a poem that is of its own time, which in Milton's case meant a poem of the experience of defeat.

While Henry Fielding was writing *Tom Jones* (1749), he was also producing weekly newspapers (*The True Patriot* and *The Jacobite's Journal*) attacking the Jacobites, who in 1745 had marched from

Scotland in an attempt to restore the Stuart monarchy that had been summarily removed in 1688.

Sir Walter Scott's novels of Scottish history were written at a time when Scotland no longer existed as a separate political entity.

Thomas Moore, the son of a Dublin grocer, was one of the most popular and influential poets in the fashionable London society of the Regency, but his *Irish Melodies* (1808–34) were written in celebration of an Ireland that no longer existed as a separate political entity. They were conceived contemporaneously with a satirical poem called *Intolerance* (1808), in which Moore offered a plea for a more humane treatment of the Irish.

James Joyce's *Dubliners* (1914) was published when Dublin was a colonial outpost, whereas his *Ulysses* (1922) was published in the year that Dublin became the capital of a free state – though the book appeared in Paris, and Joyce concluded it with a colophon marking it as a work of exile ('Trieste-Zurich-Paris 1914–1921').

Omitted from my list of 'United Kingdom' Nobel Laureates was a citizen of Saint Lucia, Derek Walcott, born 1930, prize awarded 1992, 'for a poetic oeuvre of great luminosity, sustained by a historical vision, the outcome of a multicultural commitment'. Over the centuries since 1500, his West Indian island was passed several times between the colonizing grasp of the French and the British. The language and subject matter of Walcott's poetry is shaped by a mixed heritage of the indigenous, the English and the French:

> Pomme arac,
> otaheite apple,
> pomme cythère,
> pomme granate,
> moubain,
> z'ananas

the pineapple's
Aztec helmet,
pomme,
I have forgotten
what pomme for
the Irish potato,
cerise,
the cherry,
z'aman
sea-almonds
by the crisp
sea-bursts
au bord de la 'ouvrière
Come back to me,
my language.
Come back,
cacao,
grigri,
solitaire,
ciseau
the scissor-bird
no nightingales
except, once...

('Sainte Lucie', in *Sea Grapes*, 1976)

The nightingale has warbled through English poetry from medieval lyric to Milton to Keats to T. S. Eliot. Walcott introduces other species of bird. Since the 19th century, the English have been forced to make room for refugees from the blight of the Irish potato. Now the English orchard apples of Keats and Hardy are joined by sweet Caribbean fruit.

Saint Lucia was only granted independence from the United Kingdom in 1979, so for much of Walcott's career he was a British colonial subject. His poetry, like Naipaul's prose (for all the differences of stance between the two writers), is deeply imbricated with the English literary tradition, even as he brings it into dialogue with the language, outlook, and environment of his own small island. And in *Omeros* (1990), he follows in the footsteps of such Englishmen as George Chapman (translation of the *Odyssey*, 1614–15), Alexander Pope (translation of the *Odyssey*, with assistance from William Broome and Elijah Fenton, 1725–6), and Alfred Lord Tennyson ('Ulysses' as poem, 1842), not to mention T. E. Lawrence 'of Arabia' (translation of the *Odyssey*, 1935) and James Joyce of Dublin (*Ulysses* as novel), by absorbing a foundational narrative of Western literature into his own place, his own imagination. Achille and Philoctete become working fishermen among the Windward Islands instead of warrior heroes of antiquity.

English journeys

'English' has to be measured against 'British', 'Scottish', 'Welsh', and 'Irish'. English Literature is also interested in the interplay between home and abroad, the islands and the continental mainland, the homeland and the empire, the attitude of people from the old country to the most important colony that is no longer theirs, the United States of America. Charles Dickens' *Martin Chuzzlewit* (1844) caused great offence for its treatment of the latter theme.

'There is a world elsewhere' says Shakespeare's Coriolanus, on being banished from Rome, the ancient state that was such a formative influence on the British ruling class, courtesy of their classical education. Travel, exploration, exile, cosmopolitanism: these have been among the great themes of English writing. But, like the opposition between England and Britain/Ireland, the dialectic of home and abroad, or the centre of power and the outposts of empire, creates distortions of its own. It implies that England is a homogenous place. But it is not. From Daniel Defoe (*A Tour through the Whole Island of Great Britain*, 1724–7), to

William Cobbett (*Rural Rides*, 1830), to H. V. Morton (*In Search of England*, 1927), J. B. Priestley (*English Journey*, 1934), and George Orwell (*The Road to Wigan Pier*, 1937), journalists have gone on the road and discovered a wealth of different Englands, rural and urban, sleepy and raucous, ordered and broken, hedgerows white with hoar frost and tenements black with coal dust, all rich in raw material for the observant eye.

Writers are not always nationalists or spokespeople for 'one nation' – or even if they are, like Benjamin Disraeli, who became prime minister on precisely this ticket, their arguments in favour of 'one nation' come from their knowledge that there are, as Disraeli put it in the subtitle to his novel *Sybil* (1845), *Two Nations*. For Disraeli, the two nations were the rich and the poor; for Elizabeth Gaskell, they were *North and South* (1855), the opposing worlds of industrial labour and leisured gentility. The two nations take many forms. Dissenting traditions have been as formative of 'Englishness' as orthodox 'patriotism'. There is a long tradition of appeal to an 'other England', an 'authentic' national identity – often symbolized by such figures as Robin Hood – that has been corrupted or displaced by state power. The opposition of Saxon against Norman frequently recurs here: though written by a Scotsman, *Ivanhoe* had an immense influence on 19th-century images of what it meant to be English.

So too with the Saxon and the Celt. As Oxford Professor of Poetry in the 1860s, Matthew Arnold argued that Celtic literature offered a corrective to what he called the Philistinism of the Anglo-Saxon temperament embodied in English middle-class life. He suggested that the romantic characteristics of English Literature – 'its turn for style, its turn for melancholy, and its turn for natural magic, for catching and rendering the charm of nature in a wonderfully near and vivid way' – all had their origins in Celtic sources. In Arnold's account, Shakespeare's greatness lay in his blending of English pragmatism with 'an openness and flexibility of spirit, not English'.

Among the principal creative oppositions upon which English Literature is built are court versus county and country versus city, 'green and pleasant land' versus 'dark Satanic mills'. This is both a literary and a political formation: in the 18th and 19th centuries, Toryism was grounded in the country, landowning interest, Whiggism and later Liberalism among the newly prosperous urban mercantile class (though plenty of individuals could be cited as exceptions to this rule).

There is a long tradition of urban writing in England: Elizabethan satirists such as John Marston and John Donne attacked fashion-conscious young city gentlemen in pursuit of pleasure and preferment. They were abetted in the process by their own status as young gentleman of precisely this kind. City comedy became a notably popular theatrical form in the early 17th century. The naïve country girl or backwoods squire coming to town became a stock type in Restoration and 18th-century comedy. Conversely, in novels such as Jane Austen's *Mansfield Park*, urban sophisticates (Henry and Mary Crawford) disrupt the life of a settled rural estate. The psychogeography of London is the unifying motif of an exceptionally dark and powerful group of late 20th-century novels: Michael Moorcock's *Mother London* (1988), Martin Amis's *London Fields* (1989), Iain Sinclair's *Downriver* (1991), Peter Ackroyd's *The House of Doctor Dee* (1993). A post-apocalyptic London is the favoured setting of dystopian fiction from Richard Jefferies' *After London* (1885) to J. G. Ballard's *The Drowned World* (1962) and Will Self's *The Book of Dave* (2006).

The tradition of anatomizing the capital city goes back to the ancient Roman satirist Juvenal. Indeed, Dr Johnson's poem 'London' is an 'imitation' or free adaptation of Juvenal's third satire. In its turn, the idealization of the rural estate in contrast to the fevered world of the court goes back to the poetry of Horace, but it departs further from him than the counter-tradition does from Juvenal. Where Horace's farm is a generic place of retreat, English rural poetry is steeped in geographic specificity and local affection. It is of a piece with the distinctively English taste for landscape painting in watercolour, for local history and county loyalty, for picturesque tourism.

Dr Johnson defined topographical verse as 'local poetry, of which the fundamental object is some particular landscape ... with the addition of ... historical retrospection or incidental meditation.' The foundation-text of the genre was Sir John Denham's *Cooper's Hill*, in which the poet climbs a hill near Egham in Surrey and looks down on Windsor (cue praise for King Charles I and his forebears), Thames (hail the empire-builders who sailed thence and made 'both *Indies* ours'), and Runnymede (where Magna Carta was signed, laying the foundation of English liberty). First published in 1642, Denham's poem became an underground Royalist classic during the Cromwellian era. It influenced a long sequence of 18th-century 'prospect' poems in which a well-ordered landscape became symbolic of the supposedly natural hierarchies of society. By the end of the century, poetic paeans to the sturdy English oak had been attached to the vision of the organic State that was articulated most eloquently by Edmund Burke in his *Reflections on the Revolution in France* (1790). William Wordsworth initially challenged the politics of the genre by replacing national history with personal memory (as in 'Tintern Abbey') and peopling his landscapes with the poor and the dispossessed (as in 'Michael' and 'Resolution and Independence'), but his retreat to the Lake District was a sign of his rejection of radical politics. At the beginning of the 20th century, the rural 'Georgian' poets were characterized by nostalgia and complacency; the future belonged to the urban modernists. Then in their anti-modernist allegiance to the rural muse of Thomas Hardy, the major English poets of the second half of the 20th century revealed themselves to be deep-rooted conservatives: Philip Larkin complained that the countryside had been overrun by caravan sites, Geoffrey Hill yearned elegiacally for a 'Platonic England' of 'cedar and soft-thudding baize' ('The Laurel Axe' in 'An Apology for the Revival of Christian Architecture in England', 1978), and Ted Hughes as Poet Laureate tried to revive the mystique of the monarchy.

So the story goes. But, like all reductively political readings of literature, this narrative is a gross over-simplification. The nostalgia of landscape poetry is usually conservative with a small 'c' in that it idealizes an older way of life that is threatened or lost – but that perhaps never really existed. Precisely the same may be said of urban satire. But the impulse behind the sentiment is ultimately more to do with the poet's sense of him- or herself as an exile from Eden than with any party political allegiance. The land of lost content is really the writer's own past, the innocence of childhood, the place where we began.

The melting pot

In 1908, a new play by the English-Latvian-Polish-Jewish writer, public speaker, and Zionist activist Israel Zangwill opened in Washington, DC. Greeted with enthusiasm by President Theodore Roosevelt, it was about a Russian-Jewish family that has emigrated to the United States in order to escape a pogrom. At one point, the central character says 'America is God's Crucible, the great Melting-Pot where all the races of Europe are melting and reforming . . . Germans and Frenchmen, Irishmen and Englishmen, Jews and Russians – into the Crucible with you all! God is making the American'. The title of the play, *The Melting Pot*, was taken up as shorthand for the supposedly unique destiny of America as a new country in which immigrants were welcome and could begin a new life regardless of their ethnic origin.

But is that destiny so unique? For two millennia, Britain has been a crucible into which Celts, Romans, Anglo-Saxons, Norsemen, Normans, Huguenots, Dutch, Hanoverians, Jews, migrants, refugees, and former colonial subjects, all the races of Europe and far beyond, have melted and reformed. By bringing their own languages, they have immeasurably enriched the English language, and that is one of the principal sources of the unique richness and variety of English Literature.

Early in the 17th century, the Anglo-Italian dictionary-maker John Florio translated the essays of the Frenchman Michel de Montaigne into English, importing a wealth of new words and phrases that left a deep mark on the later writings of William Shakespeare. In the 20th century, the Irishmen James Joyce and Samuel Beckett reinvented English literary language with unprecedented ingenuity (in Joyce's case) and exactitude (in Beckett's). Caribbean and British-Caribbean poets such as Edward Kamau Brathwaite and Linton Kwesi Johnson have reanimated English poetry by means of a language culled from their own vernacular. In the very act of rebelling against the 'tradition', they have become part of it, modifying the whole existing order in exactly the way described by Eliot. The 'new word order' of Linton Kwesi Johnson is dependent on dialogue with his poetic inheritance:

> if I woz a tap-natch poet
> like Chris Okigbo
> Derek Walcot
> ar T. S. Eliot
>
> I woodah write a poem
> soh dyam deep
> dat in bittah-sweet
> like a precious
> memari
> whe mek yu weep
> whe mek yu feel incomplete...
> (from *Mi Revalueshanary Fren: Selected Poems*,
> Penguin Classics, 2002)

'Alien' writers question and revalue the tradition, because it belongs to a history in which their own people have been oppressed. But at the same time, they 'naturalize' themselves, often by expressing a sense of gratitude and obligation – it is the English writers of the past who have given them the equipment and the will to find their own voice. This is one of the very few matters on which the 20th century's two most wide-ranging Trinidadian writers – left-wing historian, essayist, and cricket writer C. L. R. James, and right-wing novelist, polemicist, and travel writer V. S. Naipaul – would unhesitatingly agree.

Derek Walcott drives along the contested margin between England and Wales, Anglo-Saxon and Celt. When he writes of his 'dispossession', the reader's first instinct is to assume that he is making a simple reference to imperialist or racist oppression. But he is not:

> Sometimes the gusts of rain veered like the sails
> of dragon-beaked vessels dipping to Avalon
> and mist. For hours, driving along
> the skittering ridges of Wales, we carried the figure
> of Langland's Plowman on the rain-seeded glass ...
>   ... We had crossed into England –
> the fields, not their names, were the same ...
> The sun brightened like a sign, the world was new
> while the cairns, the castled hillocks, the stony kings
> were scabbarded in sleep, yet what made me think
> that the crash of chivalry in a kitchen sink
> was my own dispossession?
>
>   (Walcott, *Midsummer*, 1984, poem XXXV)

The poet laments, as Edmund Burke did at the time of the French Revolution, that the age of chivalry is gone. Writers no longer dream with misty eyes of Arthur's return from the blessed isle of Avalon. Instead, modern literature looks back in anger. In 1954, the critic David Sylvester wrote an article called 'The Kitchen Sink', an allusion to a painting by John Bratby, who sought to introduce the banality and boredom of everyday life into English art. The term 'kitchen-sink realism' was soon applied to the plays and novels of the 'Angry Young Men' who turned literature in the same direction, the most famous example being John Osborne's *Look Back in Anger*, staged at the Royal Court in 1956, the year of the Suez crisis that marked the turn of the tide against the British empire.

Chivalry versus kitchen sink replays the old battle between romance and realism. Walcott is an epic and lyric poet, and a dramatist who found not banality but beauty in the voices of his native Saint Lucia. His allegiance is divided: he is the guardian of romance, and yet romance has been diminished by the very democratization of art that has enabled him, a sometime colonial subject, to become that guardian. Even as he marks himself as an outsider, who is merely driving through the border landscape rather than dwelling within it, he lays claim to the inheritance both of Arthurian romance and of a tradition of lyrical English dissent that goes back to the vision of a 14th-century English ploughman poet on the nearby Malvern Hills.

Walcott is on a midsummer pilgrim's progress into his cultural inheritance. In the previous poem, he has heard the ghosts of Shakespeare's Justice Shallow and Justice Silence in the voices of old men in the garden of a timber-framed pub in Warwickshire. Witnessing a landscape 'scabbarded' in what George Orwell in *Homage to Catalonia* called 'the deep, deep sleep of England', he discovers that he has been possessed by his reading. The poet does not cease from mental fight, nor does the pen sleep in his hand. He tracks the feet that in ancient times walked upon England's mountains green. Langland's feet, Milton's, Bunyan's, Blake's. He keeps alive their vision of a new earth, a new Jerusalem, now and in English Literature.

11. 'And did those feet' in its original context: William Blake, Preface to *Milton: A Poem* (1804–11), prophesying a 'New Age' in which England will become the 'New Jerusalem'

Publisher's acknowledgements

Further reading

Chapter 1

On children's literature: Seth Lerer, *Children's Literature: A Reader's History from Aesop to Harry Potter* (Chicago, 2008).

Juliet Dusinberre, *Alice to the Lighthouse: Children's Books and Radical Experiments in Art* (Basingstoke, 1987).

Jacqueline Rose, *The Case of Peter Pan: or the Impossibility of Children's Literature* (Basingstoke, 1984).

On Kipling: David Gilmour, *The Long Recessional: The Imperial Life of Rudyard Kipling* (London, 2002).

Chapter 2

F. R. Leavis on *Hard Times*: in his *The Great Tradition* (London, 1948).

Eliot on tradition: essays in his *Selected Prose*, ed. Frank Kermode (London, 1975).

Semiotics: *A Roland Barthes Reader*, ed. Susan Sontag (London, 1982).

Orwell on literature: *The Penguin Essays of George Orwell* (London, 1994).

The 'canon': Frank Kermode, *The Classic* (London, 1975).

John Guillory, *Cultural Capital: The Problem of Literary Canon Formation* (Chicago, 1994).

Margaret Ezell, *Writing Women's Literary History* (Baltimore, 1993).

Chapter 3

Heaney: *Stepping Stones: Interviews with Seamus Heaney by Denis O'Driscoll* (London, 2008).

Celts: James Carney, 'Language and Literature to 1169', in *A New History of Ireland I: Prehistoric and Early Ireland*, ed. Dáibhí Ó Cróinín (Oxford, 2005), pp. 451–510.

Ossian: Fiona Stafford, *The Sublime Savage: A Study of James Macpherson and the Poems of Ossian* (Edinburgh, 1988).

The Celtic twilight: Ben Levitas, *The Theatre of Nation: Irish Drama and Cultural Nationalism 1890–1916* (Oxford, 2002).

Old English literature: Malcolm Godden and Michael Lapidge (eds.), *The Cambridge Companion to Old English Literature* (Cambridge, 1986).

Alfred the Great: *Asser's 'Life of King Alfred' and Other Contemporary Sources*, tr. Simon Keynes and Michael Lapidge (Harmondsworth, 1983).

After the Conquest: Laura Ashe, *Fiction and History in England 1066–1200* (Cambridge, 2007).

The 14th century: James Simpson, *The Oxford English Literary History*, Volume 2: *1350–1547: Reform and Cultural Revolution* (Oxford, 2002).

Chaucer: *The Cambridge Companion to Chaucer*, ed. Piero Boitani and Jill Mann, 2nd edn. (Cambridge, 2004).

The Bible: Robert Carroll and Stephen Prickett, Introduction to *The Bible: Authorized King James Version* (World's Classics edition, Oxford, 1997).

Northrop Frye, *The Great Code: The Bible and Literature* (London, 1982).

Frank Kermode, *The Sense of an Ending: Studies in the Theory of Fiction* (Oxford, 1967).

Chapter 4

Rhetoric: Brian Vickers, *In Defence of Rhetoric* (Oxford, 1989).

Enlightenment Scotland: Robert Crawford, *The Scottish Invention of English Literature* (Cambridge, 1998).

Empire and English studies: Gauri Viswanathan, *Masks of Conquest: Literary Study and British Rule in India* (New York, 1989).

Auto-didacts: Jonathan Rose, *The Intellectual Life of the British Working Classes* (New Haven, 2001).

Criticism and the public sphere: Jürgen Habermas, *The Structural Transformation of the Public Sphere: An Inquiry into a Category of Bourgeois Society* (1962; tr. Thomas Burger, Cambridge, Mass., 1991).

Terry Eagleton, *The Function of Criticism: From 'The Spectator' to Post-Structuralism* (London, 1984).

Karen O'Brien, *Women and Enlightenment in Eighteenth-Century Britain* (Cambridge, 2009).

Stefan Collini, *Public Moralists: Political Thought and Intellectual Life in Britain: 1850–1930* (Oxford, 1993).

Dr Johnson: Freya Johnston, *Samuel Johnson and the Art of Sinking, 1709–1791* (Oxford, 2005).

Romantic critical theory: M. H. Abrams, *The Mirror and the Lamp: Romantic Theory and the Critical Tradition* (New York, 1958).

Coleridge: Seamus Perry, *Coleridge and the Uses of Division* (Oxford, 1999).

Hazlitt: Tom Paulin, *The Day-Star of Liberty: William Hazlitt's Radical Style* (London, 1998).

Textual questions: John Jowett, *Shakespeare and Text* (Oxford, 2007).

Philip Gaskell, *From Writer to Reader: Studies in Editorial Method* (Oxford, 1978).

David Greetham, *Textual Scholarship: An Introduction* (London, 1994).

D. F. McKenzie, *Bibliography and the Sociology of Texts* (Cambridge, 1999).

Jerome McGann, *A Critique of Modern Textual Criticism* (Charlottesville, 1992).

Chapter 5

Periodization and the history of literary forms: Alastair Fowler, *A History of English Literature* (Cambridge, Mass., 1987).

Renaissance: Richard Helgerson, *Forms of Nationhood: The Elizabethan Writing of England* (Chicago, 1992).

David Loewenstein and Janel Mueller (eds.), *The Cambridge History of Early Modern English Literature* (Cambridge, 2003).

Romanticism: Duncan Wu (ed.), *Romanticism: A Critical Reader* (Oxford, 1995).

Nicholas Roe (ed.), *Romanticism: An Oxford Guide* (Oxford, 2005).

Modernism: Chris Baldick, *The Oxford English Literary History*,
    Volume 10: *1910–1940: The Modern Movement* (Oxford, 2004).

Hugh Kenner, *The Pound Era* (Berkeley, 1971).

Helen Carr, *The Verse Revolutionaries: Ezra Pound, H. D. and the
    Imagists* (London, 2009).

The line of Hardy: Donald Davie, *Thomas Hardy and British Poetry*
    (London, 1973).

Rival traditions in modern poetry: Randall Stevenson, *The Oxford
    English Literary History*, Volume 12: *1960–2000: The Last of
    England?* (Oxford, 2004).

Chapter 6

Kinds of poetry: Paul Fussell, *Poetic Meter and Poetic Form* (New York,
    1965; revised edn. 1979).

Elegy: G. W. Pigman III, *Grief and English Renaissance Elegy*
    (Cambridge, 1985).

The shadow of war: Paul Fussell, *The Great War and Modern
    Memory* (Oxford, 1975).

Donne: John Carey, *John Donne: Life, Mind and Art* (London,
    1990).

John Stubbs, *John Donne: The Reformed Soul* (London, 2006).

Multiple meanings in poetry: William Empson, *Seven Types of
    Ambiguity* (London, 1930) and *The Structure of Complex Words*
    (London, 1951).

Chapter 7

Shakespeare: Jonathan Bate, *Soul of the Age: The Life, Mind and
    World of William Shakespeare* (London, 2008).

King Lear: Stanley Cavell, 'The Avoidance of Love', in his *Disowning
    Knowledge in Seven Plays of Shakespeare* (Cambridge, 1987).

Metadrama: Anne Righter (Barton), *Shakespeare and the Idea of the
    Play* (London, 1962).

Shakespeare in print: Lukas Erne, *Shakespeare as Literary
    Dramatist* (Cambridge, 2003).

Lamb and limits of the stage: J. W. Donohue, *Dramatic Character
    in the English Romantic Age* (Princeton, 1970).

Shakespeare as inspirer and inhibitor: Jonathan Bate, *The Genius of
    Shakespeare* (London, 1997).

Comedy: Alexander Leggatt, *English Stage Comedy, 1490–1900: The Persistence of a Genre* (London, 1998).

Michael Cordner, Peter Holland, and John Kerrigan (eds.), *English Comedy* (Cambridge, 1994).

Chapter 8

Romance and novel: Paul Hunter, *Before Novels: Cultural Contexts of Eighteenth Century English Fiction* (New York, 1990).

Geoffrey Day, *From Fiction to the Novel* (London, 1987).

18th-century fiction: Ian Watt, *The Rise of the Novel* (London, 1957).

Michael McKeon, *The Origins of the English Novel, 1600–1740* (Baltimore, 1988).

Women and Gothic: Sandra Gilbert and Susan Gubar, *The Madwoman in the Attic: The Woman Writer and the Nineteenth Century Literary Imagination* (New Haven, 1980).

Austen: Claudia Johnson, *Jane Austen: Women, Politics, and the Novel* (Chicago, 1988).

Novel and nation: Patrick Parrinder, *Nation and Novel: The English Novel from its Origins to the Present Day* (Oxford, 2006).

Condition of England: Raymond Williams, *Culture and Society 1780–1950* (London, 1958).

Catherine Gallagher, *The Industrial Reformation of English Fiction: Social Discourse and Narrative Form, 1832–1867* (Chicago, 1985).

Victorian fiction: Philip Davis, *The Oxford English Literary History*, Volume 8: *1830–1880: The Victorians* (Oxford, 2002).

Dickens: Michael Slater, *Charles Dickens: A Life Defined by Writing* (New Haven and London, 2009).

Comic fiction: Glen Cavaliero, *The Alchemy of Laughter: Comedy in English Fiction* (Basingstoke, 1999).

Modernism and stream of consciousness: Robert Humphrey, *Stream of Consciousness in the Modern Novel* (Berkeley, 1962).

David Lodge, *Consciousness and the Novel* (Cambridge, Mass., 2002).

Sterne and narrative technique: Wayne Booth, *The Rhetoric of Fiction* (Chicago, 1961).

Gerard Genette, *Narrative Discourse: An Experiment in Method* (Ithaca, 1983).

Further reading

Chapter 9

Englishness: Paul Langford, *Englishness Identified: Manners and Character 1650–1850* (Oxford, 2000).

David Gervais, *Literary Englands: Versions of 'Englishness' in Modern Writing* (Cambridge, 1993).

Alison Light, *Forever England: Femininity, Literature and Conservatism between the Wars* (London, 1991).

Ireland: Declan Kiberd, *Inventing Ireland: Literature of the Modern Nation* (London, 1995).

The British Question: Hugh Kearney, *The British Isles: A History of Four Nations* (Cambridge, 1995).

Linda Colley, *Britons: Forging the Nation 1707–1837* (London, 1992).

Norman Davies, *The Isles: A History* (London, 1999).

John Kerrigan, *Archipelagic English: Literature, History and Politics 1603–1707* (Oxford, 2008).

Murray Pittock, *Celtic Identity and the British Image* (Manchester, 1999).

Empire: Edward Said, *Culture and Imperialism* (London, 1993).

Bill Ashcroft et al. (eds.), *The Empire Writes Back: Theory and Practice in Post-Colonial Literature* (London, 1989).

Paul Gilroy, *The Black Atlantic: Modernity and Double-Consciousness* (London, 1993).

Country and city, region and landscape: Raymond Williams, *The Country and the City* (London, 1973).

Jonathan Bate, *The Song of the Earth* (London, 2000).

Immigrant writers: Bruce King, *Oxford English Literary History*, Volume 13: *1948–2000: The Internationalization of English Literature* (Oxford, 2004).

Graham Huggan, *The Post-Colonial Exotic: Marketing the Margins* (London, 2001).

Index

English Literature